Cooking for Yourself for the First Time

Help Has Arrived
120 Easy, Healthy Recipes

Nancy N. Wilson

Cooking for Yourself for the First Time

Help Has Arrived
120 Easy, Healthy Recipes

By Nancy N Wilson

© Blurtigo Holdings, LLC
Published May 2019 in the United States of America
Under the title: *Single, On-your-own and Hungry*

Republished with the new title May 2020
ISBN: 978-1-7330941-7-7

Disclaimer and Terms of Use: The Author and Publisher have strived to be as accurate and complete as possible in the creation of this book. While all attempts have been made to verify information provided in this publication, the Author and Publisher assume no responsibility for errors, omissions, or contrary interpretation of the subject matter herein. Any perceived slights of specific persons, peoples, or organizations are unintentional.

Images

DEDICATION

*This cookbook is for young, singles everywhere
who are creating their path in the world.
Since eating is a necessity, why not enjoy it?*

*The recipes we have included will make your life easier and more
enjoyable whether you are preparing a meal to share or savoring
your creations by yourself.*

Thank You

... for buying my book.
If you enjoy it, please take a minute and
post a review on Amazon and Goodreads or
any other platform where you purchased the book.

For a complete list of my published cookbooks,
please, visit my Author's Page on Amazon.

http://amazon.com/author/nancywilson

Nancy N. Wilson

https://MamasLegacyCookcooks.com
https://NancyNWilson.com

Please help me continuously improve my books.
If you find errors or omissions or have a problem with a recipe,
please, contact me immediately at wilsonemarketing@gmail.com
so I can make the necessary corrections.

Table of Contents

Introduction

Welcome to the world of being single and on-your-own!

It's possible that practically everything in your life has changed since you moved into your first apartment, except for one important thing - *you must eat!*

For many, the transition into preparing your meals as a single adult may be simply something you enjoy and embrace. Maybe you grew up cooking at your mom's side and eventually spread your wings at home and became a great cook in your own right.

For others, it may be just the opposite. Maybe you were so busy with a myriad of activities that cooking was never something that captured your interest. You now realize that you know nothing about planning, shopping, and preparing meals.

Either way, this book, *Cooking for Yourself for the Frist Time* is a gold-mine of possibilities with 120 easy, healthy recipes. If you are in the "I can't cook" group, it will be a gift from Heaven.

Since 2012, I have been researching the best methods for cooking healthy meals and collecting healthy recipes, then, sharing what I learned through my cookbooks.

I was feeling good about the number of cookbooks I had published until one day I realized that there are very few cookbooks available for young cooks – those who are just learning to cook or young adults who are single and on-their-own for the first time in their lives. I began to wonder who was helping them with the important skill of learning to prepare healthy foods for themselves, and in the future for their families?

I shifted my direction slightly and created two new cookbooks. One for _Tweens and Teens_ and this book for all of you who are **_Cooking for Yourself for the First Time_**.

I began collecting delicious recipes for all types of meals and a variety of snacks and desserts. Most of the recipes are quick and easy to prepare. A few are more complicated (but, still easy) and will be good choices if you want to entertain and impress.

For the most part, the recipes call for healthy, natural products – in other words, you will create the dishes from scratch and the result will be nutrient-rich foods that you will thoroughly enjoy.

You will not only enjoy eating the delicious meals, snacks, and desserts, you will also be supplying your mind and body with the nutrients needed to function on the highest level.

For your convenience, calorie count per serving has been provided for most recipes. Use it as a guide. The number may not be exact depending on your choice of ingredients. This will be helpful for those of you who count calories, as I do.

For the novice cooks, I also included a section on **_Kitchen Safety Tips_** to help you develop good habits while cooking, which will make all the difference in your cooking experience; and, another section on **_Basic Cooking Tools for Success in the Kitchen._**\

I learned long ago that everything is easier when you have the right tools for the job. You can start collecting them now – a few pieces at a time. Soon you will have everything you need. My guess is that you will keep most of them for a long time because they will become indispensable in your kitchen.

Cooking can be great fun, creative, and extremely fulfilling. It is a life adventure that never ends. Live – Cook – Eat – Enjoy!

Kitchen Safety Tips

Dress for Cooking

1. Wear clean, snug clothes with tight, short sleeves – nothing loose and dangling that can catch fire.

2. Wear an apron to protect your clothes – there will always be spills and splashes.

3. Keep long hair securely tied back so you don't get hair in your food and there is no danger of it catching fire.

Always Work with Clean, Dry Hands

1. Clean, dry hands are critical in food safety.

2. Washing your hands is always the first step before touching any food or appliance and repeat, as needed, during the cooking process. Unwanted germs in the food you are preparing can make people sick.

3. Wash your hands with soap after handling raw meat – especially chicken.

4. Rinse your hands as necessary to keep them clean and dry – wet hands can be slippery.

Keep a Clean, Tidy Kitchen

1. *Clean as you go* by wiping counters and cleaning up spills when they happen. This will keep the area sanitary, non-slippery, and clear so you have plenty of space to work.

2. Put ingredients away as soon as you use them.

3. The first two practices make kitchen cleanup much quicker when you are finished cooking.

4. Close cabinet doors and drawers completely so you don't bump into them and hurt yourself.

Learn to Use Appliances Correctly

1. Be sure the stovetop is clear before turning on a burner.

2. Check electrical cords on portable appliances to be sure they are in good condition (no breaks or frayed cords).

3. Keep all portable electrical appliances away from water so you don't get shocked.

4. Keep electrical cords away from the stovetop, oven, and sink.

5. Don't plug in an appliance if your hands are wet.

6. When you have finished cooking and before you leave the kitchen, be sure that small appliances are stored properly, and the oven and stove-top burners are turned off.

Protect Yourself from Burns

1. It is easy to get burned in the kitchen, so it is critical to know how to avoid burns and to know what to do if it happens.

2. Never cook with dangling sleeves, loose clothing, or loose long hair that can catch fire. This is even more important when cooking on a gas stovetop.

3. When using the oven, pay attention to all parts of the oven so you do not accidentally burn yourself as you put pans in or take them out of the oven.

4. Always use hot pads/potholders when handling and carrying hot pans and when removing pans from the oven and microwave.

5. Never add water to a pan that has hot oil in it. The oil will splatter and burn anyone near the stove.

6. If you burn yourself, quickly run cold water over the burned area (rubbing it with a big ice cube also works).

7. When stirring something in a pot on the stovetop, be sure to hold the handle with your non-dominant hand to prevent the pot from slipping off the burner and spilling, burning anyone nearby, including you.

8. When letting something simmer on the stovetop, always turn pot handles toward the back of the stove so that no one can bump into them and knock over the pot.

Manage the Risk of Fire

1. Keep paper towels, dish towels, and potholders away from the range top so they don't catch on fire.

2. Have a fire extinguisher in the kitchen and know how to use it.

3. Never use water on a kitchen fire, it may make the fire bigger. If the fire is small, it can be put out with baking soda or smothered with a lid.
4. If the fire turns into leaping flames, leave the house and call 911 immediately.

Learn How to Use Knives Correctly

1. Watch where and how you are cutting.
2. Never cut toward your body or your hand. Always cut away from your fingers and body.
3. Don't put knives or other sharp objects in a sink full of water.
4. Always use sharp knives - a sharp, clean knife is a safe knife. Most kitchen knife accidents come from trying to cut with a dull knife.
5. Store knives in a knife block.
6. Hold sharp knives correctly
7. Pinch Grip - Professional chefs will almost always promote holding a knife with a pinch grip where the thumb and forefinger pinch the bottom of the blade. It allows for control and steadies the hand when cutting.
8. Pointer Grip - Place an index finger along the top of the knife, which will steady your hand. This is usually easier for smaller hands. If you are safe and have good control of the knife, use the technique that is the most comfortable. I suggest practicing both techniques and see what comes naturally to you.

Use the Claw Technique to Cut Safely

Always use a common safety technique is called "The Claw." It is simple and natural. For example, you would hold a tomato with your non-dominant hand by curling your hand into a claw-like shape, with the fingernails holding the food. You will keep your hand in this position to stabilize the food and away from the knife, which limits the risk of a serious injury.

Practice safe cutting techniques with fruits and vegetables like bananas, cucumbers, and peppers.

Stand Up Straight

This will keep you balanced, alert, and focused while using a knife or any other cutting tool.

Handle Food Properly

1. Always work with clean hands.
2. Always use clean plates and utensils.
3. Never put fresh vegetables or cooked food on an unwashed plate or cutting board
4. Always cut meat and chicken on a cutting board and wash thoroughly with hot soapy water when you are finished.
5. Cooking is a wonderful skill to develop. Learning to do it safely is of primary importance. Safety is the kitchen is something that should always be practiced regardless of your age and experience.

Basic Cooking Tools
for Success in the Kitchen

Set of Mixing Bowls

Pyrex Glass Mixing Bowl
Set

Measuring Cups &
Spoons

U-Taste 10 Piece
Measuring Cups and
Spoons Set

Liquid Measuring Cups

Anchor 77940 3-Piece
Measuring Cup Set

Wooden Cutting Board

Organic Bamboo Cutting
Board with Juice Groove -
Anti Microbial

Handheld Electric
Mixer

BLACK+DECKER 6-
Speed Hand Mixer

Set of Wooden Spoons

Wooden Spoons Set for
Cooking

Wire Whisk	Rubber Spatula	Pancake Turner

OXO Good Grips 11-Inch Better Balloon Whisk	M KITCHEN WORLD Heat Resistant Silicone Spatulas Set	Dexter-Russell Pancake Turner, Stainless Steel with Walnut Handle

Sharp Cutting Knives	Chef Knives	Vegetable Peeler

Tovla Children's Cooking Knives	Mercer Culinary Renaissance 6-Piece Forged Knife Block Set,	OXO 20081 Peeler, Swivel, Black

Dutch Oven	Small (1-egg) Frying Pan	Griddle

Lodge 6 Quart Enameled Cast Iron Dutch Oven	GreenPan Mini Ceramic Non-Stick Round Egg Pan	Farberware Nonstick Aluminum 11-Inch Square Griddle

Cast Iron Frying Pan

Lodge 12 Inch Pre-seasoned Cast Iron Skillet with Red Silicone Hot Handle Holder

Spring-form Baking Pan

Nordic Ware Leakproof 9-inch Springform Pan

9 X 13-inch Baking Pan

Pyrex Glass Oblong Baking Dish

8-Inch Square Baking Pan

Pyrex Basics 8.1" Square

Cookie Sheets (2)

Wilton 2105-0109 Perfect Results Non-Stick Mega Large Cookie Pan

9-inch Pie Plate

Pyrex Glass Bakeware Pie Plate 9" x 1.2" Pack of 2

6-Well Muffin Pan

Wilton Non-Stick 6-Cup Standard Muffin Pan, 2 Pack

12-Well Muffin Pan

Wilton Non-Stick Muffin Baking Pan, 12-Cup

Pie Crust Edge Protector

Baking Pie Crust Protector Shield for 9-inch Pies

Cookie Scoops	Pastry Wheel Cutter	Microwave Cooking Plate for Bacon

Norpro Stainless Steel Cookie Scoops, Set of 3	Double Pastry Wheel	Joie Piggy Microwave Bacon Tray with Splatter Lid

QUICK & EASY BREAKFAST

To eat – or not eat – breakfast? That is the question. There is no solid evidence that supports the habit of eating breakfast jump-starts your metabolism or helps you lose weight.

However, ***I believe breakfast is important.*** You should eat something – a piece of fruit, whole-grain toast with peanut butter, or a glass of freshly squeezed juice. Keep in mind that you have been fasting for 7 - 9 hours while you were asleep, and the body needs nutrients for energy and water for hydration.

There are also studies that show:
- The body's blood sugar control is better in the morning; so, eating breakfast results in lower average daily blood sugar levels.
- People with Type 2 Diabetes who don't eat until lunchtime will have increased blood sugar levels after eating lunch and dinner.

The conclusion regarding breakfast is that anyone struggling with blood sugar levels (hypoglycemia or Type 2 Diabetes) should eat a healthy breakfast.

For all other adults (not children), if you are not hungry in the morning, it is not a disaster if you skip breakfast; but . . . make sure that you drink water to stay hydrated and eat healthy foods for the rest of the day.

On the other hand, . . . if your body says, "I'm hungry" – don't ignore the signals. Take the time to EAT (healthy food, of course).

You must decide what works for you and what will be the most helpful in reaching your goals. Regardless of the choice you make, use the following as your mantra:

When you are hungry, EAT!

When you are full, STOP!

When you are thirsty, DRINK water!

Avocado Toast

1 serving – Total calories depend on the type of bread used

Avocado toast is creamy, crisp, and delicious. It is a quick, easy, healthy breakfast, or a yummy snack! When preparing any dish with avocado, keep in mind that it will turn brown quickly. So, prepare and serve immediately.

INGREDIENTS

- 1 thick slice of your favorite bread
- ½ ripe medium avocado (130 calories)
- Salt and pepper
- Extra toppings of your choice (optional)

EXTRA TOPPINGS

- Sliced cherry tomatoes
- Finely chopped onions
- Salsa (mild, medium, or hot)
- Fried, scrambled, or poached egg

DIRECTIONS

1. Cut the avocado in half and remove the pit.
2. Carefully scoop the avocado from the peeling into a small bowl.
3. Mash it with a fork until it is smooth (you can leave small chunks if you like).
4. Add a little salt (about ⅛ teaspoon) – start with a little and add more to taste.
5. Toast the bread the way you like it.
6. Spread avocado on top of your toast.
7. Sprinkle lightly with pepper (optional).
8. Enjoy every bite with just the avocado – or add extra toppings.

Banana Egg Pancakes

1 serving of four 5-inch pancakes – 255 Calories w/o toppings

These delicious pancakes are filled with healthy goodness. Yummy when sprinkled with powdered sugar or topped with butter and honey or pure maple syrup.

INGREDIENTS

- 1 ripe banana mashed
- 1 cage-free egg
- 2 tablespoons half and half (or milk)
- ¼ cup pancake flour
- Dash of salt

DIRECTIONS

1. In a small mixing bowl, mash the banana until mushy.
2. Add egg and milk.
3. Beat with a fork or wire whisk until fluffy.
4. Add pancake flour and dash of salt.

5. Beat again until flour is mixed in completely.
6. Heat griddle until medium-hot.
7. Coat griddle lightly with butter.
8. Pour small amounts of batter onto griddle – makes four pancakes. *(Or cook as one large pancake on the griddle or in a small round frying pan. This is also delicious but a little more difficult to flip.)*
9. Cook on the first side until bubbles start to form and edges are cooked.
10. Flip the pancake and continue cooking until the second side is lightly browned.
11. Lower the heat, if necessary, to prevent burning.

RECIPE NOTES

- For extra protein and additional flavor, add 1 tablespoon real peanut butter to the batter.

Ham and Egg Bird's Nest

6 Servings – 157 Calories per serving

This is a fun and healthy breakfast that you can cook for the family. They will love it. Add hot buttered toast and a dish of strawberries for a complete meal.

INGREDIENTS

- Softened butter *(to grease the muffin cups)*
- 6 thin slices of ham
- 6 cage-free eggs
- 6 teaspoons salsa *(optional)*
- ¾ cup grated cheese *(Colby-Jack, Cheddar, or Parmesan)*
- 3 green onions, finely sliced
- Salt and pepper, to taste

DIRECTIONS

1. Preheat oven to 350° F.
2. Grate the cheese and chop the onions.
3. Lightly grease each muffin cup with butter.
4. Line each muffin cup with a ham slice, so that it creates a nice nest for the egg.
5. Bake at 350°F for 5 minutes.
6. Remove the pan from the oven and crack one egg into each cup.
7. Salt and pepper, to taste.
8. Top with salsa, grated cheese, and sliced green onions.
9. Return to oven and bake for 12 minutes more.
10. Check doneness of eggs – if OK, remove from oven. If not, continue to bake for one minute at a time until done to your liking.
11. Slip each nest onto a plate and serve.

RECIPE NOTES

- If you do not like spicy foods, don't use the salsa.

Healthy Crunchy Granola

12 Servings of ½ cup each – 337 Calories per serving

This is a healthy easy-to-make, gluten-free granola filled with spice and nuts. It is tasty for breakfast as cereal with milk or yogurt, or for eating alone as a snack.

INGREDIENTS

- 3 cups quick or old-fashioned oats
- 1 cup chopped pecans *(almonds/walnuts/pine nuts)*
- 1 cup pepitas *(shelled pumpkin seeds)*
- ¼ cup wheat germ
- ½ cup dried cherries or cranberries
- 1 teaspoon ground cinnamon
- ½ teaspoon salt
- 1/8 teaspoon ground cloves
- 1/8 teaspoon nutmeg
- 1 teaspoon vanilla extract

- 1/3 cup organic honey
- ¼ cup oil (melted coconut or canola)

DIRECTIONS

1. Preheat oven to 350° F.
2. Place a silicone baking mat or parchment paper on a large cookie sheet and set aside.
3. Place all dry ingredients *except the dried cranberries or cherries* in a large bowl; set aside.
4. Place the honey, oil, and vanilla in a small bowl and stir to combine.
5. Pour the mixture over dry ingredients and stir lightly until dry ingredients are well coated with the wet ingredients.
6. Spread the mixture evenly onto the prepared baking sheet.
7. Bake in preheated oven for 30 minutes (stir carefully after 15 minutes).
8. Watch carefully during the last 15 minutes – bake only until granola is light golden brown.
9. Remove from oven and stir in the dried cranberries or cherries – be sure to mix thoroughly.
10. Cool completely and store in an airtight container in the pantry for up to two weeks or in the freezer for up to two months.

RECIPE NOTES

- If you like sweeter granola, you can add 3 tablespoons of brown sugar to the dry ingredients.

Microwave Bacon

2 Servings (2 slices each) – 140 calories per serving

This is an easy, safe way to cook bacon. It typically takes 1 minute per strip of bacon to cook well (not crispy). The cooking time can vary. Watch carefully because it can get too crispy very quickly.

INGREDIENTS

- 4 slices naturally cured bacon *(no nitrates)*

DIRECTIONS

1. Layout slices side-by-side on a microwave-safe cooking plate lined with a paper towel – or use clean, doubled paper towels.
2. Cover with lid or a clean paper towel to keep grease from splattering.
3. Microwave on high for 2 minutes – check for doneness.
4. Microwave 30 seconds to 1 minute longer until done to taste.
5. Serve at once.

Overnight Oatmeal

1 serving - 362 Calories per serving (with no extras)

Try this easy, protein-packed, healthy, delicious breakfast. You can make it at night, cover, and place in the fridge. Voilà! Add a little fruit and a touch of cream or milk and is ready to enjoy in the morning before rushing off to work.

INGREDIENTS

- ⅓ cup oats
- Dash of salt
- ⅓ cup whole milk or half-and-half
- ⅓ cup plain Greek yogurt
- 1 or 2 teaspoons organic honey
- 1 tablespoon chia seeds or wheat germ *(optional)*
- Large dash of cinnamon *(optional)*

Extras you can add for flavor and fun:

- Diced bananas or strawberries
- Sliced grapes
- Whole blueberries
- Chopped nuts *(sliced almonds, pecans, and walnuts are good)*
- Heaping teaspoon peanut or almond butter

DIRECTIONS

1. Place all the ingredients (except extras: fruit/nuts/etc.) in a cereal bowl or pint jar.
2. Stir well until the mixture is completely blended and smooth.
3. Cover with foil or lid, and place in the fridge until morning.
4. When ready to have breakfast, add the extras *(fruit/nuts/etc.)*, a little more milk, stir well, and enjoy every bite.
5. Bacon is a tasty side dish.

Scrambled Eggs with Cheese

1 serving – 263 Calories per serving

This recipe is scrambled eggs at their best. Try them, you will love them. Delicious with a couple of strips of bacon and warm, buttered toast.

INGREDIENTS

- 1 teaspoon butter
- 2 fresh cage-free eggs
- 1 tablespoon half-and-half
- Salt and pepper
- 2 heaping tablespoons shredded cheese

DIRECTIONS

1. Set the shredded cheese where you can reach it easily.
2. Crack eggs into a small mixing bowl.
3. Add half-and-half *(or milk)*.
4. Beat with wire whisk until eggs are fluffy.
5. Sprinkle with a little salt and pepper.
6. Place a frying pan on the stove over medium heat.
7. When the pan is hot, spread the butter evenly over the bottom of the pan.
8. Pour the egg mixture into the pan.
9. Stir continuously with a wooden spoon (be sure to go around the edges and across the bottom of the pan so it stays evenly scrambled).
10. When eggs are cooked the way you like them, remove the pan from the stove, add cheese and gently fold into the eggs.
11. Scrape the eggs onto your serving plate and breakfast is ready.
12. Buttered toast with jam, a glass of freshly squeezed orange juice, and a couple of strips of bacon makes it a complete meal.

TRADITIONAL BREAKFAST

PANCAKES/WAFFLES

FRENCH TOAST

Quick, easy breakfasts are perfect for mornings when you must get up and rush off to work or school. But, there are lazy mornings when you have time to fix your favorite, old-fashioned breakfast that reminds you of days gone by.

This section covers all those perfectly wonderful comfort foods that everyone loves. They are not only good for a leisurely breakfast, but they can be equally wonderful for dinner.

Be sure to use healthy ingredients like whole-wheat flour and protein-enriched pancake flour whenever possible.

Serve fresh fruit as toppings or as a side dish to get that extra serving of fruit for the day; plus, it adds color, flavor, and texture to your meals.

Blueberry Buttermilk Pancakes

4 Servings – 497 Calories per serving (w/o syrup or sugar)

The tang of buttermilk goes a long way in making pancakes better and brighter. Always use fresh blueberries and adjust the amount to your taste.

INGREDIENTS

- 2 cups flour
- 2 teaspoon baking powder
- 1 teaspoon baking soda
- ½ teaspoon kosher salt, or slightly less table salt
- 3 tablespoons sugar
- 2 large cage-free eggs, lightly beaten
- 3 cups buttermilk
- 4 tablespoons unsalted butter, melted, plus 1 tablespoon extra for brushing griddle.
- 1 cup fresh (or frozen) blueberries

31

DIRECTIONS

1. Preheat an electric griddle to 375° F. or place a griddle or cast-iron skillet over medium-high heat.

2. Place the flour, baking powder, baking soda, salt, and sugar in a medium bowl and mix with a wire whisk.

3. Add the eggs, buttermilk, and 4 tablespoons melted butter, and whisk to combine. The batter should have small lumps – don't overmix.

4. Test the griddle or frying pan by sprinkling a few drops of water on it. If the water bounces and spatters, the griddle is hot enough. If it is smoking, let it cool a bit before adding the batter.

5. Using a pastry brush, brush the remaining ½ teaspoon butter onto the griddle. Wipe off the excess with a folded paper towel.

6. Using a ½ cup measuring cup *(for a 6-inch pancake),* pour the batter in pools 2 inches apart.

7. If you wish to make blueberry pancakes, either stir them into the batter or arrange a small handful over the cooking pancake, pressing them in slightly.

8. When the pancakes have bubbles on top and are slightly dry around the edges, about 2½ minutes, flip over. If any batter oozes or blueberries roll out, push them back under with your spatula.

9. Cook until golden on bottom, about 1 minute.

10. Repeat with the remaining batter. You can keep the finished pancakes on a heat-proof plate in the oven at 175° F.

11. Serve warm, buttered, and sprinkled lightly with powdered sugar or warm pure maple syrup.

Chocolate French Toast

6 Servings – 348 calories per serving

This is a wonderfully special Sunday breakfast. . . . and tasty enough for an unusual dessert. It is a chocolate surprise that you or anyone you serve will love.

INGREDIENTS

- 3 large eggs
- 1 cup whole milk
- 1 teaspoon sugar
- 1 teaspoon vanilla extract
- ¼ teaspoon salt
- 12 slices day-old bread, crusts removed
- 3 milk chocolate candy bars *(1.55 ounces each),* halved
- 2 tablespoons butter
- Powdered sugar

DIRECTIONS

1. In a large bowl, whisk the eggs, milk, sugar, vanilla, and salt.
2. Pour half of the mixture into an ungreased 13 X 9-inch baking dish.
3. Arrange six slices of bread in a single layer over egg mixture.
4. Place one piece of chocolate in the center of each piece of bread.
5. Place the last 6 bread slices on top and cover evenly with the remaining egg mixture.
6. Let stand for 5 minutes.
7. Melt butter over medium heat in a large non-stick skillet.
8. Place chocolate sandwiches in skillet and toast until golden brown on both sides.
9. Cut sandwiches diagonally in half.

10. Sprinkle lightly with powdered sugar.

11. Serve immediately with bacon and fresh fruit.

RECIPE NOTES

- Substitute six 1-ounce squares of bittersweet or semisweet chocolate for the milk chocolate candy bars.

- Heat squares in the microwave for 10 seconds before cutting into smaller pieces to place on the bread.

- Chocolate chips would also work in a pinch; but, keeping them contained in between the two slices of bread can be tricky.

French Toast Par Excelance

4 Servings (2 slices each) - 329 Calories per serving (without toppings)

If you want a truly scrumptious breakfast that is filled with rich flavors and textures, this is it! A glass of freshly squeezed orange and your favorite hot coffee make this the perfect meal to treat yourself on Sunday morning before the long work week begins.

INGREDIENTS

- ¾ cup half-and-half
- 4 large cage-free eggs
- 1 tablespoons honey *(warmed in the microwave for 20 seconds)* or 1 tablespoon sugar
- ½ teaspoon vanilla *(use with sugar - not with honey)*
- ¼ teaspoon salt
- 8 slices hearty bread *(fluffy white does not work well)*
- 4 tablespoons butter

DIRECTIONS

1. In a medium-size mixing bowl, whip the half-and-half, eggs, honey, and salt *(use a good wire whisk or an electric hand mixer)*.

2. When ready to cook, pour the mixture into a 9 X 9-inch baking dish; set aside.

3. Preheat oven to 375° F.

4. Dip bread into the egg mixture, and soak for 30 seconds on each side.

5. Remove slices to a wire rack that is sitting in a sheet pan, and allow to sit for 1 to 2 minutes *(this step is optional but worth a try)*

6. Place 1 tablespoon of butter in a 10-inch non-stick sauté pan over medium heat.

7. When butter is melted and spread evenly in the pan, place 2 slices of bread at a time into the pan and cook until golden brown, approximately 2 to 3 minutes per side.

8. Remove from pan and place on rack in oven for 5 minutes. Repeat with all 8 slices.

9. Serve immediately with lots of real butter and toppings: maple syrup, powdered sugar, whipped cream, jam, or fresh fruit *(lightly sweetened if you choose)*.

RECIPE NOTES

- Milk can be substituted for half-and-half, but you will miss the additional richness that the cream provides.
- Substantial white bread: white country loaf, brioche, or challah bread. A family favorite is Dave's Killer Bread with seeds and nuts. Try different kinds to find your favorite. I have used King's Hawaiian® Sweet Round Bread *(use less sweetener for this one)*.
- If the bread is a day or two old, it works better.

Old-Fashioned Pancakes

4 Servings – 233 Calories per serving (without syrup)

Our family loves pancakes for breakfast or dinner! You can eat these scrumptious pancakes with lots of butter and hot syrup or dress them up with sweetened strawberries and whipped cream. Or – toss a few chocolate chips into the batter and dribble with chocolate syrup and a dollop of sour cream. The possibilities are endless.

INGREDIENTS

- 1 large cage-free egg
- 1 cup buttermilk
- 2 tablespoons butter, melted
- 1 cup flour

- 1 tablespoon sugar
- 1 teaspoon baking powder
- ½ teaspoon baking soda
- ½ teaspoon salt
- ½ teaspoon vanilla

DIRECTIONS

1. Place eggs in a medium-sized bowl and beat with a whisk until foamy.
2. Add remaining ingredients in the order listed.
3. Beat until the mixture is smooth – but don't overmix.
4. Heat griddle on medium-high heat while mixing batter.
5. Grease the griddle with 1 teaspoon butter.
6. Pour or spoon batter onto the hot, buttered griddle.
7. Each pancake should be approximately 4 inches in diameter.
8. Turn pancakes as soon as they are puffy and full of bubbles, but before the bubbles break.
9. Cook the second side until golden brown.
10. Serve with lots of real butter, real maple syrup, honey, sour cream, powdered sugar, or your favorite jam.

VARIATIONS

Cornmeal Pancakes

- Decrease flour to a ½ cup and add ½ cup cornmeal. *(Try this crunchy variation – it's very tasty. I discovered this secret when I was in grad school.)*

Apple Pancakes

- Decrease buttermilk to ½ cup and stir ½ cup applesauce into the batter.

Sausage Gravy and Biscuits

4 Servings – 537 Calories per serving (with 2 biscuits)

This may very possibly be the best breakfast in the world! Don't worry about the calories. It is an indulgence you cannot miss. It is a must-have for cowboys of all ages and will likely become one of your favorites as well – it is certainly one of mine.

INGREDIENTS

- ½ to 1 lb. breakfast sausage, hot or mild *(If you like a lot of sausage in your gravy, use 1 lb. I like less, so my choice is ½ lb. Fix it both ways to see which you prefer.)*
- ¼ cup flour, more if needed
- 1 can evaporated milk *(add enough water to make 2 cups)*, plus extra whole milk if needed
- ¼ teaspoon seasoned salt, plus more regular salt, to taste
- 1 teaspoon freshly ground black pepper, more to taste

- 1 batch homemade buttermilk biscuits *(An easy choice is to make them from Bisquick®) or use Anna's® Homegrown Flaky Biscuits (found in the refrigerated section of the grocery store.)*

DIRECTIONS

1. Break sausage into small pieces – make a single layer in large heavy skillet.
2. Stir and brown the sausage over medium-high heat until it is no longer pink.
3. Sprinkle flour onto sausage, reduce heat to medium-low, and stir until flour coats all the sausage – add a little extra, if needed.
4. Continue to stir and cook for another minute.
5. Slowly add the milk, stirring constantly.
6. Continue cooking, stirring frequently, until gravy thickens – up to 10 minutes.
7. Stir in the seasoned salt and freshly ground pepper.
8. Continue cooking until thick and scrumptious.
9. If it thickens too fast, add ½ cup whole milk.
10. Taste and adjust the seasoning, it may need a little more salt.
11. Spoon the sausage gravy over warm biscuits – fresh from the oven.
12. Serve immediately with freshly squeezed orange juice and hot coffee.

Whole-Wheat Buttermilk Pancakes

4 Servings – 298 Calories per Servings

Whole-wheat flour and buttermilk combine to make a hearty, healthy, light pancake with a slight tang.

INGREDIENTS

- 1 cup whole-wheat flour
- ¼ cup regular flour
- ¼ cup yellow cornmeal
- 1 teaspoon baking powder
- ½ teaspoon salt
- ¼ teaspoon baking soda
- 1½ cups buttermilk
- 2 large cage-free eggs, lightly beaten
- 2 tablespoons honey *(or 1 tablespoon sugar and ½ teaspoon vanilla)*
- 1 cup fresh (or frozen/thawed) berries (optional) *(blueberries, raspberries, or sliced strawberries)*

DIRECTIONS

1. Butter griddle or large heavy skillet.
2. Combine whole-wheat flour, regular flour, cornmeal, baking powder, salt, and baking soda in a large bowl.
3. Combine buttermilk, eggs, and honey *(or sugar and vanilla)* in a medium-size bowl.
4. Add buttermilk mixture to flour mixture with a wooden spoon; stir until blended but still a little lumpy.
5. Heat prepared griddle over medium heat until hot.
6. Pour 1/3 cup batter onto the griddle.
7. Cook for 2 to 3 minutes on each side or until golden brown.
8. Repeat with remaining batter, until all batter has been used.
9. Serve with real butter, warm maple syrup, or lightly sweetened berries.

VARIATION

- Sugar the berries and let them stand for 15 minutes.
- Stir well, spoon onto the pancakes, and top with a generous serving of real whipped cream.

Yummy Waffles

4 to 6 Servings – 595 Calories per serving (if serving 4)

This is a traditional (and delicious) choice for Sunday breakfast, but also great at night for a casual meal when served with bacon and eggs.

INGREDIENTS

- 3 large cage-free eggs
- 1¾ cups flour
- 1¾ cups milk
- ¼ cup butter, melted
- ¼ cup of vegetable oil
- 4 teaspoons baking powder
- ½ teaspoon salt
- 1 tablespoon sugar
- ½ teaspoon vanilla extract

DIRECTIONS

1. Preheat waffle iron.
2. Separate eggs – eggs in large bowl and whites in a smaller bowl.
3. Beat egg yolks in a large bowl with whisk until fluffy.
4. Add flour, milk, butter, oil, sugar, baking powder, salt, and vanilla - beat with an electric hand mixer just until smooth. Do not stir excessively.
5. Beat egg whites until stiff and *fold* into batter.
6. Pour approximately ½ cup batter onto hot waffle iron (use more batter if using a large waffle iron).
7. Cook until golden brown.
8. Serve hot with lots of butter and favorite toppings: warm maple syrup, powdered sugar, or jam.

RECIPE NOTES

*   You can keep the batter covered in the refrigerator for up to a week. Just be sure to whisk the batter well before making the pancakes. You may need to add a little milk to thin it down.
*   You can substitute whole wheat flour for white flour.
*   You can also use pancake mix or Bisquick® - following the directions on the package with the following notes: Be sure to make with milk and add the same amount of butter, sugar, and vanilla as required in this recipe.

LET'S DO BRUNCH

Inviting friends over for a relaxing. delicious brunch that you have prepared is a wonderful way to spend a leisurely weekend morning.

Sharing good food, dreams for the future, and lots of laughter can be a welcome break after a hectic week of classes or time in the office. *(And . . . it gives you a chance to show off your cooking skills.)*

Such times spent together will strengthen your bonds of friendship and build cherished memories that will last a lifetime.

Bacon, Egg & Mushroom Casserole

8 Servings – 338 Calories per serving

A lovely twist on a traditional breakfast - that will easily serve eight. Great for brunch! Invite your friends over soon.

INGREDIENTS

- ½ cup butter (1 cube)
- 8 oz fresh white mushrooms, sliced
- ½ lb. thick-cut bacon, diced *(Use good quality bacon – preferably pepper-cured without nitrates.)*
- ½ cup flour
- Salt and freshly ground pepper
- 1-quart milk
- 12 large cage-free eggs, lightly beaten
- ¾ cup half-and-half
- ¼ teaspoon salt – adjust to taste
- Fresh chives, finely chopped for garnish

DIRECTIONS

1. Pre-heat oven to 350° F.
2. Butter a 9-inch glass soufflé dish.
3. Sauté mushrooms in 2 tablespoons butter over medium-high heat - until lightly browned, about 3 minutes.
4. In a large heavy skillet, cook the bacon and drain on paper towels.
5. Discard the grease and use the same frying pan for the next step.
6. Add 4 tablespoons of butter to the skillet, add the cooked bacon *(except a little saved for garnish)*, and ¾ quarters of the mushrooms.
7. Sprinkle with flour, salt, and pepper and stir well.

8. Gradually stir in the milk and cook, stirring constantly until the mixture is thick and smooth. - about 20 minutes.

9. Cover and set aside.

10. Melt remaining 2 tablespoons butter in a separate skillet over medium-low heat.

11. Place eggs, cream, and ¼ teaspoon salt in a bowl - beat until frothy.

12. Pour into the hot skillet with the butter and cook until ***very softly*** scrambled - DO NOT overcook.

13. In the buttered soufflé dish, alternately layer the scrambled eggs and the bacon white sauce, ending with sauce.

14. Top with the remaining mushrooms and reserved bacon.

15. Bake uncovered until heated through - 15 to 20 minutes.

16. Garnish with chopped chives.

Baked Breakfast Feast

6 Servings – 657 Calories per serving

Everything is cooked in one pan. Just put it together, bake, and serve. Add a big bowl of fruit salad, plus a warmed, pre-sliced French baguette with real butter – what a treat!

INGREDIENTS

- (20-ounce) package organic hash-brown potatoes
- 2 tablespoons unsalted butter, melted
- 1 tablespoon olive oil
- ¼ teaspoon dried thyme
- ¼ teaspoon dried basil
- ¼ teaspoon dried oregano
- ¼ teaspoon garlic powder
- Salt and freshly ground black pepper, to taste
- 1 cup shredded cheddar cheese
- 12 slices bacon (no nitrates)
- 6 large cage-free eggs
- 3 tablespoons Parmesan cheese, freshly grated preferred
- 2 tablespoons fresh chives, finely chopped

DIRECTIONS

1. Preheat oven to 400° F.
2. Lightly grease a baking sheet with butter or spray with nonstick spray.
3. Place hash-browns in a large mixing bowl.
4. Stir in butter, olive oil, thyme, basil, oregano, and garlic powder and gently toss to combine.

5. Season with salt and pepper, to taste.

6. Spread seasoned potatoes evenly onto the prepared baking sheet.

7. Sprinkle cheese evenly over the top.

8. Place in oven and bake until the edges are lightly browned ~ 20 to 25 minutes.

9. Remove from the oven and create six wells in the potatoes for the eggs.

10. Place bacon slices evenly on the top, leaving the wells open.

11. Crack the eggs into the wells – be careful so you do not break the yolks.

12. Sprinkle eggs with Parmesan cheese.

13. Season with salt and pepper, to taste.

14. Place in oven and bake until the egg whites have set, and bacon is cooked through - approximately10-12 minutes more.

15. Sprinkle chives lightly over the top.

16. Serve immediately with fresh orange juice, warm toast, and sweet butter.

Ham and Cheese Casserole

8 Servings - 417 Calories per serving

You'll find everything you want for breakfast in this satisfying casserole – potatoes, eggs, cheese, and ham. This is an excellent main course dish for brunch, especially when served with fresh fruit and garlic bread.

INGREDIENTS
- 4 medium-large potatoes, thinly sliced
- Salt and pepper to taste
- 4 cup cheddar cheese, shredded
- 1 lb. fully cooked ham, cut in small cubes
- 7 large cage-free eggs

51

- 1 cup milk
- ½ teaspoon salt
- ½ teaspoon dry mustard
- Chopped green onions for garnish

DIRECTIONS

1. Peel and slice potatoes very thin.
2. In a heavy frying pan, heat 1 tablespoon each of butter and vegetable oil.
3. When the oil is hot, added sliced potatoes and fry until tender and nicely browned; lightly salt and pepper the potatoes.
4. Turn often so potatoes do not burn.
5. Place cooked potatoes in a single layer in a buttered 13 x 9-inch baking dish.
6. Sprinkle with cheese and ham.
7. In a bowl, beat eggs, milk, salt, and mustard - pour over ham.
8. Cover and bake at 350° F for 1 hour.
9. Uncover; bake 15 minutes longer or until edges are golden brown and a knife inserted near the center comes out clean.
10. Sprinkle chopped green onions as garnish.

RECIPE NOTES

- You can substitute 1 (20 oz) package of organic hash-browns for the potatoes and proceed from Step 4. *(The casserole is tastier if you fry your potatoes as directed in the recipe.)*

LUNCH

SOUP, SALAD, and SANDWICHES

When I was growing up, the mid-day meal (dinner) was the main meal of the day. It usually included a hot and tasty entrée.

The evening meal was "supper." The recipes in this section – for LUNCH - would have been similar to our choices for the last meal of the day.

Lunch can be a quick bite – hopefully, something healthy – or it can be a little more elaborate.

Be sure to check-out Easy Healthy Packed Lunches, which we included to make it easy for you.

Have fun preparing and enjoying the dishes, whether it is a packed lunch for work or school, a grab-and-go to eat as you commute, or a nice sit-down meal with a partner, roommates, or visiting friends.

The important thing is that you eat lunch.

You need the sustenance to keep your energy up for the second half of the day. If you skip lunch and hunger sets in with a vengeance, it is too easy to succumb to the temptation of high-fat, sugary vendor food. Be smart and eat a hearty, healthy lunch.

Easy Healthy Packed Lunches

It is a good idea to use airtight, *microwave-safe* containers when you pack a lunch. There is a good selection of containers available through *Amazon*. They come in all shapes and sizes – including the little condiment cups with lids.

Some are stackable, some have separate compartments or sections. Some even have special freezer sections for keeping your lunch cool if you can't refrigerate it.

You should also pick up a package of disposable forks and knives, plus a carrying bag. Be sure you get one that is big enough for your needs.

Quick-Fix Lunch Ideas

NOTE: Anything with mayonnaise, meat, or dairy must be kept cool.

- A dish of cottage cheese with sliced berries, grapes, pears, peaches, or banana and a drizzle of fresh organic honey (optional) for sweetness.
- Apple slices (lightly sprinkled with lemon juice), cheese slices, and a big handful of nuts (almonds, walnuts, pecans, pistachios).
- Slices of deli meat (chicken, turkey, or ham) plus a small bag of whole-wheat Triskets® or whole-wheat crackers of choice.
- Sliced apples or celery with a serving of pure peanut butter for dipping and a couple of hard-boiled eggs with salt & pepper.
- A serving of hummus with veggies to dip (you can buy veggies prepared for this purpose).
- Two peeled, hard-boiled eggs, baby carrots, and a serving of Ranch Dressing for dipping, with a side of grapes for dessert.
- A can of your favorite sardines and a small bag of whole-wheat crackers and an apple or orange.

- A small carton of plain Greek yogurt mixed with a teaspoon of organic honey and a small carton of fresh sliced fruit ready to be mixed in.
- An individual serving of fresh guacamole (be sure it is mixed with some lime juice to keep it from going dark) with a small bag of tortilla chips. Throw in a few slices of cheese for protein and a banana or apple for dessert.
- A leg and thigh (or ½ chicken breast) from a rotisserie chicken with a small side of coleslaw, potato, or macaroni salad. (This lunch must be kept cool.)
- Sliced roasted chicken breast, sliced cheese, and a cup of fruit salad.
- Half a pita filled with avocado and chicken salad with cherry tomatoes; sliced apples on the side.
- Simple green salad (lettuce, cherry tomatoes, cucumbers) sprinkled with grated cheese – dressing of choice on the side to be added when ready to eat. A serving of fresh berries or a banana for dessert.
- Leftover fish (salmon or tilapia) on a little lettuce with sliced avocados sprinkled with lemon - black olives on the side. Fresh grapes and a dinner roll.

Don't Forget Wraps and Sandwiches

Wraps: Make them with fresh whole-wheat flour tortillas.

Sandwiches: *Dave's Killer Bread* is the healthiest choice if you can find it. If you can't, use bread with the least additives possible and made from whole grains, nuts, and seeds.
(Most of the sandwiches must be refrigerated)
- Deli ham and cheese with a little mayo.
- Deli turkey with a little mayo and a touch of raspberry jam.
- Sliced rotisserie chicken with salsa and sour cream.
- Left-over meatballs with a little sauce and cheese.

- Small chunks of rotisserie chicken and creamy avocado or guacamole.
- Healthy peanut butter (peanuts & salt only) and jam or honey.
- Egg salad, tuna salad, or chicken salad.

Useful Tips:

Don't forget to add some lettuce, chopped tomatoes, and onions. Cheese is also a tasty addition and adds protein.

You can make wraps and sandwiches as simple or elaborate as you like. Be sure they include a good portion of healthy protein.

Dinner leftovers make tasty lunches – just pack them up and reheat in a microwave. (Be sure to use microwave-safe bowls.)

If you use plastic bags, Ziplock® are the best, they keep the food fresher.

Anything with mayo, sour cream, eggs, or meat must be refrigerated to avoid food poisoning.

Best Grilled Cheese Sandwich

1 Serving – 486 Calories per sandwich

The secret ingredient in this sandwich is the mayonnaise. Don't be afraid to use it – it will not go bad because you are going to eat it immediately. Once you make a grilled cheese sandwich with mayonnaise, you will never make another grilled cheese without it.

INGREDIENTS

- 2 slices of your favorite fresh bread, *(whole wheat, sourdough or rich white bread)* Each slice should not be more than ½ inch thick
- 2 teaspoons butter (not margarine)
- 1½ tablespoon Hellmann's® or Best Foods® Real Mayonnaise
- 2 slices real Cheddar Cheese (Tillamook, Colby Jack, or Monterey Jack)

DIRECTIONS

1. Heat a heavy frying pan or griddle over medium-low heat.

2. Spread mayonnaise on one side of each slice of bread.

3. Place the cheese on top of the mayo on one of the slices and top with the 2nd slice of bread – mayo face down on the cheese.

4. Generously butter the top slice of bread and place carefully in the heated pan with the buttered side down. Place a saucer on top of the sandwich.

5. Adjust the heat so the bread sizzles gently; but, doesn't burn.

6. When the cheese looks like it is getting soft, remove the saucer and butter the top slice of bread.

7. Use a spatula to flip the sandwich over so the freshly buttered slice is now on the bottom.

8. Turn the heat down a little more and press firmly to compact the sandwich.

9. After a minute or two, turn the sandwich over several times, pressing gently after each turn, until the sandwich is compact, both sides are crusty, and the cheese is melted *(beginning to ooze out of the sides)*.

10. Place the sandwich on a plate, cut in half with a sharp knife.

11. Enjoy the tasty pleasure with a serving of potato chips and an ice-cold Coke.

Chicken and Cheese Quesadillas

2 Servings – 602 Calories per serving

Most people enjoy this Mexican-style dish. It may seem complicated the first time you make it, but you will get used to it quickly and will want to make it often.

INGREDIENTS

- 2 teaspoons very soft butter
- 4 whole-wheat flour tortillas *(8-inch)*
- 1 cup shredded cheddar cheese
- 1/3 cup onion, finely diced
- 1 large roasted chicken breast – cut in small cubes

DIRECTIONS

1. Place the soft butter in a small dish close to the stove.
2. Prepare the cheese, onions, and chicken and set those close to the stove, as well.

3. Place a griddle on the stove over medium heat.
4. Lay tortillas on clean, dry paper towels and spread soft butter all over one side of each tortilla.
5. Place two tortillas on the hot griddle (buttered side down) and sprinkle each with ½ of the cheese, onion, and chicken.
6. Top with the two remaining tortillas, buttered side up.
7. Cook over medium heat for 3-4 minutes on the first side (until lightly browned and cheese has begun to melt); and then turn carefully. *(The turning can be tricky.)*
8. Cook on the second side until it is also lightly browned.
9. Remove from heat and cut into wedges.
10. Serve with Fruit Salad or Green Salad. YUMMY!

Chicken Enchilada Soup

10 Servings – 226 Calories per serving

Chicken soup is not only good for the soul, it also warms you up on a cold winter's night. Try this wonderfully spicy variation of chicken soup.

INGREDIENTS

- 2 chicken breasts
- 1 can (25 oz) diced tomatoes
- 1 red chili pepper
- 1¼ cup of enchilada sauce
- 1 can of white beans
- 1 can of corn
- 1 onion, finely chopped
- 1 cup of water
- 1 tablespoon taco seasoning
- ½ teaspoon garlic powder

DIRECTIONS

1. Use a blender to puree the canned tomatoes until smooth.
2. Pour into a slow cooker and stir in enchilada sauce.
3. Mix in remaining ingredients and cover with the lid.
4. Cook on HIGH for about 4 hours or on LOW for about 8 hours.
5. Remove whole chicken breasts and shred them with a fork.
6. Return chicken to the slow cooker.
7. Add salt and pepper to taste.
8. Serve hot with a big basket of tortilla chips and optional toppings: sour cream, cheese, and cilantro.

Cool Coleslaw

6 Servings – 84 Calories per serving

This coleslaw will be enjoyed by all when served for dinner with hot dogs, hamburgers, or fried chicken. It is also a perfect side dish for any kind of barbeque or picnic. Even though most coleslaw recipes require time to "sit" before serving, this one can be served as soon as it is prepared.

INGREDIENTS

- ½ small head of green cabbage – chopped very fine
- 3 scallions, white parts only
- ¼ medium green bell pepper, trimmed, seeded, and coarsely grated
- ½ medium crisp, juicy apple, washed, cored, and grated or chopped very finely.
- 1 medium carrot, peeled and coarsely grated
- ¼ cup cider vinegar
- 1 teaspoon salt
- 1 teaspoon sugar
- 1/3 cup sour cream (do NOT use non-fat)
- 1/3 cup mayonnaise – Best Foods® or Hellman's® (do NOT use non-fat)

DIRECTIONS

1. Cut the cabbage into 1/8-inch shreds and cut into very thin strips or chopped into tiny pieces.
2. Place in a large mixing bowl.
3. Trim and peel the scallions and cut crosswise into very thin slices.
4. Trim, core, and grate or chop the apple.
5. Trim, peel, and grate the carrot and green pepper.
6. Add everything to the cabbage and toss to mix well.

7. Combine the vinegar, salt, sugar, sour cream, and mayonnaise in a large measuring cup and whisk until smooth.
8. Add dressing to the coleslaw and toss until everything is well-coated.
9. Serve immediately or cover and refrigerate until ready to use.

RECIPE NOTES

- If not serving immediately, cover and refrigerate – will keep up to 3 days.

Deviled Eggs

6 Servings (2 halves each serving) – 120 Calories per serving

This is a old family recipe that I hope you will enjoy. It will take a little practice to get the process down, but you will catch on quickly.

INGREDIENTS

- 2 teaspoons softened real butter
- 6 large cage-free eggs
- 2 tablespoons Hellman's® or Best Foods® Mayonnaise
- 1 teaspoon yellow mustard
- 1 teaspoon Dijon mustard
- 2 teaspoon sweet gherkin pickle juice
- ½ teaspoon sugar
- Large dash of salt and pepper
- Dash of Tabasco Sauce *(if you like it a little spicy)*
- Paprika

DIRECTIONS

1. Measure and set out the butter so it can soften.

2. Hard Boil the eggs.

    a. Place eggs in a saucepan and cover completely with water.

    b. Set on the stovetop over high heat.

    c. Let the water come to a full boil and boil for one minute.

    d. Cover with a tight lid and remove from heat.

    e. Let eggs sit in hot water for a FULL 17 minutes.

    f. Drain completely and cover with water and lots of ice.

    g. Let them sit in the ice bath until completely cool – then peel, place on a platter, cover with a light cloth or paper towel.

    h. Set aside until ready to make deviled eggs. *(If more than ½ hour, place eggs in the refrigerator.)*

3. With a sharp knife, carefully slice the eggs in half, the long way.

4. Carefully remove each yolk from the whites and place them in a medium bowl.

5. Set the egg white halves carefully back on the platter.

6. Mash the yolks with a fork.

7. Add mayonnaise, very soft butter, both mustards, pickle juice, sugar, salt, pepper, and Tabasco Sauce.

8. Mix everything with a fork.

9. Gently spoon the mixture into each egg white – forming a little mound.

10. Sprinkle with paprika.

11. If you love pickles, you can top each egg with a small chunk of sweet gherkin pickle.

12. These eggs make the perfect side dish to serve at a picnic, as an extra dish for dinner, or to eat as a healthy snack.

Fresh Fruit Salad

4 Servings – 140 Calories per serving

There is nothing quite as good as fresh fruit, especially a combination of all the best pieces – like the ones we selected. Serve the salad mixed with the honey and lime dressing or serve plain with Crème Fraiche or lightly sweetened whipped cream on the side for toppings (this is my preference).

INGREDIENTS
- 1 lb. of strawberries, stems removed and quartered
- 1 cup blueberries
- 1 cup raspberries
- 2 white peaches, or nectarines, peeled and sliced
- ½ small fresh pineapple, peeled/cored/cubed
- 1 cup seedless grapes *(black, red, or green)*
- ½ cup pomegranate arils *(for a nice crunch)*
- ¼ cup honey
- 1 teaspoon fresh lime zest

- 3 tablespoons fresh lime juice
- A few fresh mint leaves for garnish

NOTE: Experiment with other fruits and find the combination you like the best. The fruits listed in this recipe are my favorites – what will yours be?

DIRECTIONS

1. Prepare the fruit as noted above (always use organic, if possible).
2. Be sure to rinse the fruit well, especially the berries and grapes.
3. Dry off any excess water with a clean paper towel and place all the fruit in a large glass bowl.
4. Gently toss the fruit until well-mixed.
5. Whisk the honey, lime zest, and lime juice in a small bowl.
6. Add the dressing to the fruit and toss to combine.
7. Serve immediately or cover securely with plastic wrap and store in the fridge until ready to serve.
8. Before serving, stir carefully and sprinkle a few fresh mint leaves for garnish.

RECIPE NOTES

- For a delicious parfait, layer the fruit with plain Greek yogurt, lightly sweetened with honey.
- Do not zest the lime with a cheese grater – use a zester.

Grandma's Chicken Soup

8 one-cup Servings – 163 calories per serving (13 grams protein)

This healthy, tasty chicken soup comes together so quickly you will be amazed. It is good at any time of the year and especially good as a cozy dinner when it is cold outside. BTW, it is one of the healthiest dishes you can make and has been proven to have healing qualities. This one is a keeper!

INGREDIENTS

- 4 cups chicken stock
- 3 carrots, peeled and sliced
- 1 cup chopped onion
- ½ cup finely chopped celery
- 1 teaspoon dried thyme
- 2 cloves garlic, minced
- 3 *(4-ounce)* chicken breast fillets, cut into small bite-size pieces
  (Can be cut after it's cooked – or have the butcher cut it for you.)
- ½ teaspoon kosher or sea salt
- ¼ teaspoon black pepper
- ½ cup uncooked long-grain brown rice
- 1 cup frozen or fresh corn kernels
- 1 cup frozen peas
- Fresh parsley, finely chopped for garnish

DIRECTIONS

1. Add all ingredients, except corn, peas, and rice, to the slow cooker, cover and cook on low 6- 8 hours, or until carrots are tender and chicken is done.

2. If chicken were cooked whole, remove, and let it cool until you can handle it safely. Shred or cut into small pieces; then, place it back in the cooker.
3. Add rice and cook for 15 minutes more.
4. When the rice is done, add the corn and peas – continue cooking until vegetables are warm through.
5. Add additional salt and pepper to taste.
6. Serve in large soup bowls, sprinkled with finely chopped fresh parsley.
7. Serve at once with a Fresh Green Salad, hot biscuits, and real butter.

RECIPE NOTES

- Some people prefer diced potatoes instead of rice – try it both ways.
- This can also be made in a Dutch oven or a large soup kettle.
  - Place chicken, carrots, onions, celery, seasonings, and chicken broth in a large pot over high heat and bring to a boil.
  - Reduce heat, cover, and simmer for 30 minutes, skimming fat as needed.
  - Add the brown rice, reduce the heat and simmer for 1 hour. If using diced potatoes, add them the last 30 minutes.
  - Then continue from Step 3 as noted above.

Green Salad

4 Servings – 103 Calories per serving (without dressing) – 173 calories with dressing

This simple salad goes well with almost any meal – especially grilled steak, roasted chicken, and any pasta dish.

INGREDIENTS

For the Salad

- ½ small head of iceberg lettuce, shredded
- 3 or 4 leaves of romaine lettuce, shredded
- 20 cherry tomatoes, washed well, dried, and cut in half
- 2 baby cucumbers, washed well, ends removed and sliced very thin
- 1 whole avocado diced, peeling and pit removed
- Small bunch of fresh dill, minced (optional)

For the Dressing

- 2 cloves garlic, crushed
- 4 tablespoons of sour cream
- 3 tablespoons of Hellman's® or Best Foods® Mayonnaise
- A squeeze of fresh lemon juice
- Salt and freshly ground black pepper to taste

DIRECTIONS

Make the Salad

1. Rinse vegetables very carefully – be sure they are well-drained and dry before preparing for the salad.
2. Shred iceberg lettuce by cutting head in half and then, slice each half into ½ inch slices, and finally, chop into smaller pieces.
3. Place shredded lettuce in a large salad bowl.
4. Romaine lettuce: Rinse thoroughly, dry with a paper towel, and break into bite-sized pieces on top of the iceberg lettuce.
5. Baby Cucumbers: Remove most of the dark peeling and trim both ends. Then, slice into thin round slices on top of the lettuce.
6. Cherry tomatoes: Carefully cut in half and place on top of the cucumbers.
7. Avocado: Cut in half and remove the pit. Peel carefully and cut into medium-small chunks on top of the tomatoes.
8. Finely chop the fresh dill if you are using it and sprinkle into the bowl.
9. Gently toss all ingredients until well-mixed.

Make the Dressing

1. Measure and scoop the sour cream into a small bowl.
2. Add the mayonnaise.
3. Peel and crush the garlic with a garlic press and add to the mix.
4. Add squeezed lemon juice (to taste).
5. Add salt and freshly ground black pepper (to taste).

6. Mix until all ingredients are well-blended.

Note: *If you use bottled dressing check the calorie and fat content –*
both can be quite high.

RECIPE NOTES

- You can serve the salad plain as shown in the picture with dressing on the side so people can add the amount they prefer.
- Or before you serve the salad, you can pour the dressing over the salad. Then, toss it gently until all the salad ingredients are lightly covered with the dressing.

Healthy Macaroni Salad

6 Servings – 345 Calories per serving

*This easy-to-make salad is tasty all by itself. It is also an excellent choice
to serve with hamburgers or hot dogs at a picnic, a summer barbeque, or
on camping trips. Be sure to keep it well-chilled before serving. Leftover
salad should be refrigerated, as well.*

INGREDIENTS

- 1 cup dry elbow macaroni
- 4 cups of water
- Lemon juice from ½ lemon
- 3 hard-boiled, cage-free eggs, diced
- ½ cup grated cheddar cheese *(or feta cheese)*
- ½ cup celery, sliced very thin
- ½ small cucumber, peeled and diced
- 1 medium carrot, peeled and grated
- 10 cherry tomatoes, washed, dried, and cut in half
- ½ cup Hellman's® or Best Foods® Mayonnaise
- Salt and freshly ground black pepper to taste
- Dash of garlic salt

DIRECTIONS

1. Cook macaroni according to directions on the package.
2. Drain, rinse with cold water, drain again.
3. Sprinkle macaroni with lemon juice, mix well and chill in the fridge
   for 2 to 3 hours.
4. Add the rest of the ingredients, mix well, and keep refrigerated until
   ready to serve.

Homemade Potato Salad

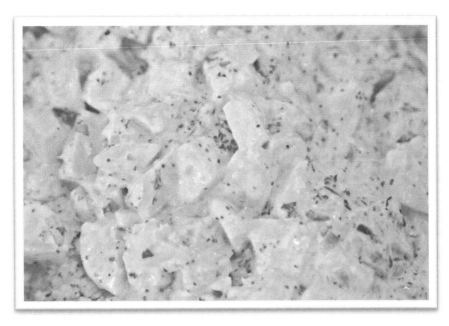

6 Servings – 277 Calories per serving

Meat and potatoes were the two basic foods when I was growing up, which meant that it was important to know how to make tasty dishes that included potatoes. This was a family favorite and is even better on the second day. Keep well-chilled when not being served.

INGREDIENTS

- 2 lbs. yellow, red, or white potatoes
- 1 tablespoon lemon juice
- ½ cup sour cream
- ¼ cup Hellman's® or Best Foods® Mayonnaise
- 1 tablespoon prepared yellow mustard
- ½ medium red onion, finely chopped *(about ½ cup)*
- 3 medium celery stalks, sliced <u>very</u> thin *(about ½ cup)*

- 3 hard-boiled eggs, peeled and chopped
- ¼ cup chopped fresh herbs *(parsley and/or cilantro)*
- Salt and freshly ground black pepper to taste

DIRECTIONS

1. Scrub the potatoes well, do not peel, and place them in a large pot.
2. Cover with at least 1½ inches of water above potatoes.
3. Season with one tablespoon of salt.
4. Place the pot over medium-high heat and bring to a boil.
5. Reduce heat to low and simmer for 15 to 20 minutes or until potatoes can be easily pierced with a fork.
6. When potatoes are done, drain completely and let cool.
7. Peel potatoes and chop into bite-sized chunks into a large bowl.
8. Sprinkle potatoes with lemon juice and salt.
9. Peel and chop the eggs on top of the potatoes.
10. Add the chopped onions, sliced celery, and herbs to the potatoes.
11. Mix sour cream, mayonnaise, and the mustard in a small bowl.
12. Add creamy mixture to the potatoes and gently stir with a wooden spoon to combine all ingredients. *(Try not to mash the potatoes.)*
13. If needed, add a little extra mayonnaise.
14. Season with salt and pepper to taste.
15. The salad will taste better if you refrigerate for at least two hours before serving. It allows the flavors to blend.

RECIPE NOTES

- Anything made with mayonnaise must always be kept cold. If it is left sitting out for an extended period, it can go bad and cause food poisoning.

Rich Carrot Soup
with Rotisserie Chicken

4 Servings (2 cups each) – 197 Calories w/o chicken; 302 calories with chicken

To stay healthy, eat lots of vegetables – everybody knows that, right? Maybe, but most people need more of them in their diet. Soup is a great way to do just that. This velvety carrot soup with roasted chicken as a condiment is perfect for lunch or dinner.

INGREDIENTS

- 1 tablespoon extra-virgin olive oil
- 2 lbs. baby carrots
- 1 medium red onion
- 1 tablespoon vinegar
- 32 ounces chicken broth
- 2 teaspoons fresh rosemary
- 1 teaspoon of sea salt

- Scant ½ teaspoon Hot Pepper Sauce *(light hand please)*
- Heavy dash of nutmeg
- ½ cup half-and-half
- 12 oz rotisserie chicken cut into small chunks, preferably white meat
- ¼ cup fresh chives or parsley, chopped

DIRECTIONS

1. Heat the oil in a Dutch oven over medium heat.
2. Add the carrots, onion, and vinegar, increase heat to medium-high, and sauté until the onion is fully softened ~ 8 minutes.
3. Add the broth, rosemary, salt, and hot pepper sauce, increase heat to high, and bring to a boil.
4. Reduce the heat to medium-low and simmer, covered, until the carrots are fork-tender, about 25 minutes.
5. Puree the soup in small batches in a blender. *(Use the "hot fill/liquid" line as a guide. Be careful. Too much hot liquid in a blender will explode.)*
6. Pour pureed soup into a large bowl.
7. Stir in half-and-half and dash of nutmeg; mix thoroughly.
8. Adjust seasoning to taste.
9. Reheat, if necessary, in the microwave.
10. Ladle soup into individual soup bowls.
11. Add a small serving *(¼ cup)* warmed chicken cubes in the center of each bowl.
12. Sprinkle with chopped chives or parsley.
13. Serve with warm French bread and real butter.

Sloppy Joes

8 Servings - 319 Calories per serving

Our family loves sloppy joes and you can make them easily with this recipe. Have plenty of hamburger buns and napkins ready. Serve with corn-on-the-cob and a crisp Green Salad. Perfect!

INGREDIENTS

- 1 tablespoon butter
- 1 medium onion, chopped
- 1 clove garlic, minced
- 1 lb. lean ground beef
- 1 *(8 ounces)* can tomato sauce
- ½ cup ketchup
- 1 tablespoon brown sugar
- 1 teaspoon ground mustard

- 1 tablespoon white vinegar
- 1 tablespoon Worcestershire Sauce
- Salt and freshly ground black pepper, to taste
- 8 hamburger buns

DIRECTIONS

1. Place one tablespoon butter in a large saucepan or Dutch oven over medium-high heat.
2. Add chopped onion and garlic.
3. Sauté until onion turns transparent and starts to brown.
4. Stir in the ground beef and cook until the meat is crumbly and no longer red ~5 minutes.
5. Spoon out any excess grease.
6. In a small bowl, place the tomato sauce, ketchup, brown sugar, mustard, vinegar, Worcestershire Sauce, ¼ teaspoon salt, and 1/8 teaspoon pepper and whisk until well blended.
7. Pour sauce over beef and stir until meat is evenly coated.
8. Cover, place over med-low heat, and simmer 20 minutes, stirring occasionally.
9. Serve on hamburger buns with sliced onions on the side for people who want them on their sloppy joes.
10. Prepare fresh corn on the cob with butter as the vegetable and a Green Salad.

EASY DINNERS

Dinner should be the best meal of the day, and it doesn't have to be a huge project. It can be a simple, easy labor-of-love – for yourself and for others who may share it with you.

It can be challenging to prepare a meal for one, but why not? You deserve to eat well. So, prepare, relax, enjoy, and save the leftovers for another day; or, freeze a couple of servings for next week. Do the work once and enjoy it more than once.

A few of the recipes will serve six or eight, which make them good choices for special occasions - when all the roommates are home, you have your family over for dinner, or you have a dinner party with friends. Surprise them with your culinary skills and willingly accept their praise.

Keep in mind that you can cut recipes in half – I do it all the time. Even if you are alone . . . preparing nice meals is great practice for the future.

Amazing Pot Roast

8 Servings – 680 Calories per serving

This one-pot meal is juicy, tender, and full of flavor. It is one of my family's primary comfort foods. The aroma as it cooks is tantalizing and creates big appetites.

INGREDIENTS

- 3 lbs. brisket or blade pot roast
- 3 tablespoons vegetable oil
- ½ cup flour
- Salt and black pepper, to taste
- 2 tablespoons Dijon mustard
- 2 tablespoons packed brown sugar
- 2 cloves garlic, crushed
- ¼ teaspoon nutmeg
- 3 large onions, sliced
- 1 cup beer or ½ cup red wine
- 1 cup beef stock or consommé
- 6 medium-large carrots, peeled and quartered
- 6 medium potatoes, peeled, and cut into 3" cubes

DIRECTIONS

1. Preheat the oven to 325° F.
2. Heat oil in a heavy, lidded roasting pan or Dutch oven.
3. Coat roast with flour on both sides.
4. Place floured roast into hot oil and brown on both sides - salt and pepper generously.
5. When the meat is browned, turn off the heat.

6.   Pour beer (or wine) and stock over top.

7.   Combine the next 4 ingredients in a small bowl, spread the mixture over roast, and layer with onions.

8.   Cover with a tight lid or heavy-duty foil and place in preheated oven for 2 hours.

9.   Add vegetables around beef, sprinkle lightly with salt and pepper - cook covered for another 1½ hours, or until roast is tender.

10. Increase oven temperature to 350° F. and remove the lid for the last 20 to 30 minutes to brown roast.

11. Remove beef and vegetables to a warmed serving platter. Cover with foil until ready to serve.

12. Mix 1 tablespoon cornstarch and cold water until blended.

13. Bring to a boil and stir in cornstarch blend to thicken juices into gravy - season to taste.

14. Serve gravy on the side.

15. Fresh crusty French bread and a crisp Green Salad make this a complete meal.

Baked Creamy Macaroni and Cheese

4 Servings – 665 calories per serving

Learning how to make comfort food that makes people feel good is important. This creamy baked mac and cheese recipe is a great place to start. It will become a favorite among friends and family.

INGREDIENTS

- 8 oz. uncooked elbow macaroni
- 1 teaspoon olive oil
- ½ stick unsalted butter
- ¼ cup flour
- ¾ cup whole milk
- 1¼ cups half and half
- 2 cups grated medium sharp cheddar cheese *(divided into 1 cup and 1 cup)*
- 1 cup grated Gruyere cheese *(divided into ½ cup and ½ cup)*.
- ¾ teaspoon salt
- ¼ teaspoon black pepper
- 1/8 teaspoon paprika

DIRECTIONS

1. Preheat oven to 325° F.
2. Butter a 9 X 9-inch baking dish; set aside.
3. Bring a large pot of salted water to a boil.
4. Add pasta to boiling water and cook one minute less than directed for al dente.
5. Drain cooked pasta and stir in one teaspoon olive oil to keep the macaroni from sticking together.

While pasta is cooking . . . Make the sauce

6. Grate both types of cheese into a large bowl.

7. Toss lightly to mix.

8. Divide into three smaller bowls
    - Approximately 1½ cups for the sauce
    - ¾ cup for the middle layer
    - ¾ cup for the top

9. Combine the milk and half-and-half in a measuring cup that has a pouring spout.

10. Melt butter in a large saucepan over medium heat.

11. Sprinkle flour over the butter and whisk to combine. It will look like very wet sand.

12. Cook for about 1 minute, whisking often.

13. Slowly pour in about 1 cup of the milk/half-and-half the mixture as you continue to cook, whisking constantly until the mixture is smooth.

14. Continue whisking as you pour in the remaining milk/half-and-half.

15. Continue whisking until the mixture is well-blended and smooth.

16. Let the mixture cook over medium heat, whisking frequently until it is very thick *(like thick gravy)*.

17. Stir in spices and ¾ cup of the grated cheeses, stirring with the whisk to combine and help the cheese melt.

18. Stir in another ¾ cup of cheese and whisk until completely melted and smooth.

Create the Casserole

19. In a large mixing bowl, place the drained pasta and cheese sauce, stir with a wooden spoon to blend thoroughly.

20. Pour half of the pasta mixture into the prepared baking dish.

21. Top with ¾ cup of grated cheeses; then, top that with the remaining pasta mixture.

22. Sprinkle the top with the last ¾ cup of cheese.

23. Bake for 15 minutes at 325° F, until cheese is bubbly and lightly golden brown.

To Make Ahead . . .

- Follow directions through step 21 and stop - **do not bake.**
- Cool completely and cover tightly with foil and refrigerate 1-2 days ahead.
- Before baking, let the dish sit on the counter for 30 minutes.
- Preheat the oven to 325° F.
- Bake for 25-35 minutes, until hot and bubbly.

For a Crunchier Topping and Firmer Consistency . . .

- Prepare recipe as directed but bake at 350° or 375° F for 20-30 minutes.
- Broil at the end of baking for approximately 2-5 minutes, until golden brown and crunchy.

Cheese Enchiladas in Red Sauce

10 Servings (1 enchilada each) – 127 Calories per serving

Enchiladas – YUM! Mexican food has always been my ethnic food of choice. How could it be anything else growing up in Southern Arizona? If you enjoy it, too. This is a recipe you will enjoy making and serving. It is easy . . . and so tasty!

INGREDIENTS

- 1 can *(28 ounces)* Las Palmas Red Enchilada Sauce
- 10 king-size corn tortillas
- 1 bunch green onions
- 12 ounces of Monterey Jack Cheese *(or Mexican cheese)*

DIRECTIONS

1. Wash, peel and chop the onions – including the greens; place them in a small bowl and set aside.
2. Pour the sauce into a medium-large saucepan and set the burner on medium-low heat.
3. Generously grease with butter a 9 X 13-inch baking pan or spray with PAM Cooking Spray.
4. Set out a large plate to use in making the enchiladas.
5. Place one tortilla in the heated sauce – be sure it is completely covered with the sauce, wait about 30 seconds or until the tortilla is limp.
6. Carefully remove the tortilla using a spoon with holes in it, so the sauce will drain back into the saucepan, and place the tortilla on the plate.
7. On one end of the tortilla, spread 1/3 cup cheese and 1 tablespoon chopped onions.

8. Starting with the filling side, roll the tortilla to form the enchilada and place it at one end of the baking dish.

9. Repeat the process until all the tortillas have been filled and placed in the baking dish.

10. After enchiladas are made, cover completely with leftover sauce.

11. Sprinkle the remaining onions and cheese on top of each enchilada.

12. Bake uncovered 30 minutes in the preheated oven.

13. Serve at once with refried beans and Mexican Rice for Mexican style dinner.

14. Serve with fresh Guacamole and sour cream for toppings.

RECIPE NOTES

- If you make the enchiladas ahead of time, cover them and place them in the refrigerator.

- DON'T put the remaining sauce on top of the enchiladas until you are ready to place them in the oven.

VARIATION

- Use hamburger seasoned with Shillings® Taco Seasoning *for the filling*, plus the onions, instead of cheese. Cheese and onions can be sprinkled on top as directed.

Chicken and Biscuit Casserole

6 Servings – 770 Calories per serving

*This excellent dinner dish takes a little time, but it will be enjoyed by all.
You can use any cooked chicken available, frozen fresh vegetables, and
Bisquick® for the biscuits, which will save a lot of time. Or, you can make
it from scratch with all the natural fresh ingredients as described in the
recipe. Either way, it is a quick, easy, and scrumptious meal.*

INGREDIENTS

For the Biscuits

- 1½ cups flour
- ¼ cup coarsely chopped fresh parsley leaves
- 1½ teaspoons baking powder
- ½ teaspoon kosher salt
- 1 cup plus 3 tablespoons cold heavy cream

For the Casserole

- 4 tablespoons unsalted butter, plus extra for greasing the baking dish
- ¼ cup all-purpose flour
- 1½ cups whole milk
- 1½ cups low-sodium chicken broth
- 3 cups cooked, shredded chicken *(about 1½ lbs. boneless chicken breast – cook it yourself or use rotisserie chicken)*
- 1 *(10-ounce)* package frozen mixed vegetables
- 2 tablespoons fresh parsley, chopped
- 2 tablespoons finely chopped fresh chives
- 1 teaspoon salt
- ¼ teaspoon freshly ground black pepper

DIRECTIONS

1. Place rack in the middle of the oven.
2. Preheat to 425° F.
3. Generously grease a 2-quart baking dish with butter; set aside.

Make the Biscuits

1. Whisk the flour, parsley, baking soda, and salt in a medium bowl.
2. Add the cream and stir with a wooden spoon until a shaggy dough is formed.
3. Refrigerate while you prepare the casserole.

Make the Casserole

1. Melt the butter in a Dutch oven or large pot over medium heat.
2. Add flour to the butter and whisk until thoroughly combined. The mixture will look like wet sand.
3. Cook until the mixture begins to dry out and turn golden-brown ~ 4 minutes.

4. Gradually whisk in a little bit of the milk until smooth, then whisk in the remainder.

5. Continuing whisking as you add the chicken broth and stir until smooth.

6. Bring to a boil, then reduce the heat and simmer, stirring constantly, until thickened ~5 to 8 minutes.

7. Remove from the heat and stir in the shredded chicken, vegetables, parsley, chives, salt, and pepper.

8. Spread the mixture evenly in the buttered baking dish.

9. Scoop out about 2 tablespoons of biscuit dough at a time and form ½ inch-thick biscuit patties

10. Place biscuits on top of the casserole.

11. Repeat with the remainder of the dough, spacing the biscuits about ½ inch apart.

12. Bake until heated through. The soup should be bubbling, and the biscuits should be golden brown ~15 to 18 minutes.

13. Set on a wire rack to cool about 5 minutes before serving.

RECIPE NOTES

- The chicken can be cooked *(poached or roasted)* one day ahead and stored in a covered container in the refrigerator until ready to use.

- Or – you can use a rotisserie chicken from the deli.

- The dish is equally tasty when served as leftovers. It can be stored in an airtight container in the refrigerator for up to 3 days.

Chicken and Egg Tostada

6 Servings – 522 calories each serving

Another Mexican-inspired recipe. These are quick and easy for a pleasant summer brunch, lunch, or light dinner. Serve with Strawberry Coolers or cold Mexican beer and enjoy a delightful meal with friends.

INGREDIENTS

- 2 tablespoons olive oil
- 2 tablespoon real butter *(not margarine)*
- 1 large clove garlic, minced
- ½ cup onion, finely chopped
- 1½ cups roasted chicken, skinned, boned, and cut into small bite-sized pieces
- 6 corn tortillas *(6" rounds)*
- 9 large cage-free eggs
- ¼ cup half-and-half
- 3 tablespoons Ortega® chopped green chilies
- ¼ teaspoon salt – adjust to taste
- Freshly ground pepper – to taste
- 1 medium can re-fried Beans *(La Sierra or El Paso Brands are good)*

TOPPINGS

- 1¼ cup Mexican cheese, shredded *(or 1 carton of Feta cheese crumbled)*
- 2 large avocados, sliced into ¼ "wedges
- 1 or 2 large tomatoes, trimmed and diced
- 1 medium white onion, finely diced
- Shredded lettuce

- 1-pint sour cream
- 1 jar salsa *(Pace's Picante is excellent)*

DIRECTIONS

Prepare Ingredients

1. Slice tomatoes and avocado, shred lettuce, chop onions, put sour cream and salsa into small serving bowls, cover vegetables with slightly damp paper towels, and keep in the refrigerator until ready to serve.
2. Sauté the onions and garlic in oil until soft, add chicken and cook until warmed through and slightly browned – keep warm.
3. Place refried beans in a glass bowl and put in the microwave – ready to heat.

Cook the Tortillas

1. Heat 1-inch of Safflower oil in a small frying pan to 365° F.
2. Fry one tortilla at a time, using tongs to turn frequently and to hold under fat until it crisps, puffs slightly, and browns lightly *(~2 minutes or less).*
3. Drain on paper towels.
4. Arrange warm, fried tortillas on two large baking sheets – three on a sheet.

Prepare the Eggs

1. Beat eggs with chilies, salt, pepper, and half-and-half.
2. Melt butter in a frying pan over medium heat, pour in the egg mixture and scramble until softly cooked. *(Eggs should still be moist.)*

Assemble the tostadas (work quickly)

1. Turn on the broiler.
2. Heat the refried beans in the microwave until warm through.

3. Spread a thin layer of beans across each tortilla and top with a thin layer of warm chicken.
4. Place a layer of scrambled egg mixture and top with shredded Mexican cheese or Feta crumbles *(try both kinds and see which you prefer)*
5. Set tray of tostadas under the broiler to melt cheese ~1 to 2 minutes.
6. Garnish each tostada with 2 or 3 avocado slices.
7. Serve immediately with side dishes of shredded lettuce, diced tomatoes, chopped onions, sour cream, and salsa.
8. Let people have a good time building their tostadas.

RECIPE NOTES
Variations

1. Fix the tostadas without the meat and serve crispy bacon strips on the side.
2. Make the tostadas with Jimmy Dean® Turkey Sausage *(9.6 oz package)*. Before you prepare the eggs . . .
    a. Cook the sausage and ½ cup finely chopped onion in 2 tablespoons oil in a large skillet over medium-high heat.
    b. Cook 8 to 10 minutes or until sausage is thoroughly cooked and crumbled, stirring frequently.
    c. Drain and keep warm until ready to assemble the tostadas.

Creamy Chicken Marsala

4 Servings – 465 Calories per serving

This creamy, delicious classic Italian dish will become one of your favorites! It is full of flavor and can be prepared in less than 30 minutes. Even though it is extremely simple, it is impressively delicious – perfect for entertaining.

INGREDIENTS

- 4 boneless skinless chicken breasts, sliced very thin
- Salt and pepper
- 2 tablespoons olive oil
- 1½ cups sliced white mushrooms
- ½ cup Marsala wine
- ½ cup chicken broth
- 1 cup heavy whipping cream
- 1 teaspoon ground mustard
- 1 teaspoon garlic powder
- Fresh parsley, finely chopped (for garnish)

DIRECTIONS

1. Place 1 tablespoon olive oil in a large skillet over medium heat.
2. Add the chicken and sprinkle lightly with salt and pepper.
3. Cook until lightly browned and cooked through. *(It doesn't take long – don't overcook.)*
4. Remove chicken and set aside on a plate.
5. Add 1 tablespoon olive oil to the pan.
6. Sauté mushrooms for 1 to 2 minutes.
7. Add the marsala wine and bring to a boil over medium-high heat for 1 to 2 minutes. *(Allows the alcohol cooks out of the sauce.)*

8. Add the chicken broth, heavy whipping cream, ground mustard, and garlic powder.

9. Bring to a boil and reduce heat and simmer for ~10 minutes or until it starts to thicken. *(If it doesn't thicken on its own, blend 1 tablespoon of cornstarch and water to make a thin liquid. Stir a little at a time into the mixture until it begins to thicken.)*

10. Place chicken back in the sauce and continue to simmer for ~1 to 2 minutes more.

RECIPE NOTES

- You can slice boneless chicken breasts in half, but it is easier to buy them thinly sliced so that they cook quickly and easily.
- The alcohol in the marsala wine burns off during the cooking process.

Creamy Garlic Linguini

4 Servings – 379 Calories per serving

This recipe is quick, easy, and oh-so-tasty. It will become a favorite for weeknights when you are tired and hungry. It can be on the table in 20 minutes. Make extra because you will enjoy the leftovers, too.

INGREDIENTS

- 8 ounces uncooked linguine or spaghetti
- 1 tablespoon butter
- 1 teaspoon flour
- 3 cloves garlic minced
- ¼ cup chicken broth
- 1 cup half-and-half
- 1/3 cup freshly grated parmesan cheese
- Salt and pepper to taste
- Chopped fresh parsley
- ½ - ¾ cup peas, corn, broccoli, (any cooked veggie you prefer)

DIRECTIONS

1. Bring to a boil a large pot of boiling water for the pasta.
2. Cook pasta al dente according to package directions.

While pasta is cooking, make the sauce.

3. Melt butter in a heavy skillet over medium-high heat.
4. Stir in the flour and let the mixture cook for 2 minutes, stirring continuously.
5. Add garlic and chicken broth, stirring until well mixed and let it simmer for about a minute.

6. Stir in cream and let the sauce cook for a few more minutes to desired thickness.

7. Stir in Parmesan cheese, and parsley,

8. Salt and pepper to taste.

9. Add veggies. if using – continue to cook until veggies are warmed through.

10. Drain the pasta and toss with the sauce until well coated.

11. If the sauce has thickened too much, add a little of the pasta water to thin it.

12. Serve immediately.

RECIPE NOTES

- Add frozen peas, corn, or mixed vegetables for color.
- You can also use chopped steamed broccoli or any favorite veggie such as carrots or chopped asparagus if they have been pre-cooked – be creative.
- For more protein, add chunks of rotisserie chicken, or a can of tuna (be sure to drain well before adding).

Creamy Turmeric Chicken

4 Servings – 401 Calories per serving

You have probably noticed that many of the dinner recipes are chicken-based. For good reason – chicken is filled with protein, it is inexpensive, it is versatile and easy to prepare. This recipe is no exception – the turmeric gives it a touch of the exotic. ENJOY!

INGREDIENTS

- 2 tablespoons unsalted butter
- 1 medium yellow onion, thinly sliced
- ¼ teaspoon freshly ground black pepper
- ½ teaspoon kosher salt, plus more for seasoning
- 1½ lbs. boneless, skinless chicken thighs
- 2½ teaspoons ground turmeric
- ½ cup dry white wine
- ½ cup heavy cream
- ½ cup low-sodium chicken broth
- Cooked basmati or jasmine rice, for serving
- Fresh cilantro leaves and tender stems, finely chopped (for garnish)

DIRECTIONS

1. Melt the butter over medium heat in a 12-inch or larger heavy skillet.
2. Add onion, 1 teaspoon ground turmeric, pepper, and ½ teaspoon of the salt.
3. Cook, stirring occasionally until the onions are softened ~5 minutes.
4. Meanwhile, place the chicken on a large plate with the smooth-top side facing up.
5. Season with a mixture of salt and 1½ teaspoon ground turmeric.

6. Lay the seasoned sided down to make a single layer in the middle of the pan,
7. Season the second side of the chicken with more salt.
8. Cook over medium heat, undisturbed, until the chicken just begins to brown, no longer than 3 to 4 minutes (any longer and the turmeric will start to burn).
9. Turn the chicken and cook for 2 minutes more.
10. Pour in the wine and use a wooden spoon to scrape the browned bits from the bottom of the pan.
11. Cook for 1 minute, pour in the cream and broth – stir gently to combine.
12. Reduce heat to medium-low, cover, and cook until the chicken is tender and cooked through ~18 to 22 minutes.
13. While chicken is simmering, cook the rice according to package directions.
14. Serve over cooked rice and garnish with cilantro.

RECIPE NOTES

- Store leftovers in a covered container for up to 3 days.

Easy Baked Penne Pasta

4 Servings – 626 Calories per serving (made with sausage)

When it is cold and you are tired – wanting some comfort food to make you feel better, what can be better than hot, cheesy, baked pasta that takes practically no effort to prepare? All you need are the ingredients, a good baking pan, a hot oven, and you are ready to go.

INGREDIENTS

- 8 ounces uncooked penne pasta (ziti also works)
- 1 can (28 oz) diced tomatoes
- 10 ounces of cooked sausage, seasoned ground beef, or left-over roasted chicken cut into small chunks
- 2 cups shredded mozzarella
- 2 cups whole milk
- 1 teaspoon finely minced garlic
- 1 teaspoon salt
- Red pepper flakes, to taste
- 1 cup shredded Parmesan cheese
- Fresh basil (optional), cut into ribbons

DIRECTIONS

1. Preheat the oven to 400° F.
2. Pour the uncooked pasta into a well-buttered, large casserole dish. *(Use a 9 X 9-inch, or 9 X 13-inch baking dish).*
3. Open the can of tomatoes and add them with their juice to the pasta - and stir.
4. Spread the meat and cheese over the top of the pasta/tomato mixture.

5.   In a separate bowl, mix the seasonings into the milk and pour over the top of the casserole.

6.   Stir gently to blend - be sure all the pasta is covered by the liquid.

7.   Cover tightly with two sheets of aluminum foil.

8.   Place in the preheated oven and bake for one hour.

9.   Remove from the oven, carefully uncover the casserole, and top with Parmesan cheese.

10. Return to the oven and continue to cook until the top is browned, and the edges are bubbling.

11. Remove from the oven, set on a wire rack to cool for at least 15 minutes. This allows time for everything firm up a bit.

12. Serve with crisp Green Salad and Garlic Bread.

13. You have the perfect dinner to warm yourself from the inside out.

Easy Macaroni and Cheese

6 Servings – 585 Calories per serving

It doesn't take long when you are cooking for yourself to learn that pasta is your best friend. There are many kinds of pasta, plus it can be prepared in a multitude of ways – most of which are quite simple. What is better than "Mac and Cheese" to make you feel warm and safe. This recipe is inexpensive, easy to prepare, and wonderful.

INGREDIENTS

- 16 ounces uncooked elbow macaroni
- ¼ cup butter (½ stick)
- ¼ cup flour
- ½ teaspoon salt
- 1 dash freshly ground pepper
- 2 cups milk (or 1 cup milk and 1 cup half-and-half)
- 2 cups shredded cheddar cheese (8 oz package shredded cheddar cheese)

DIRECTIONS

1. Cook macaroni according to package directions in a large pan of salted boiling water – cook to al dente or a little longer, if you prefer.

While macaroni is cooking . . . Make the sauce

2. In a medium saucepan, melt butter over medium heat.
3. Sprinkle flour into the butter and cook for 3-5 minutes, stirring constantly with a wire whisk.
4. Add salt and pepper, to taste.
5. Slowly add milk, stirring with a whisk after each addition.

6. Cook and stir until bubbly.

7. Add a small amount of cheese at a time, continuously stirring until cheese is fully melted.

8. Remove from heat if macaroni is not ready.

Combine Macaroni and Cheese Sauce

9. Drain macaroni, drizzle one teaspoon olive oil over the pasta and stir. This will keep the macaroni from sticking together.

10. Pour macaroni into hot cheese sauce; stir until all macaroni is well-coated.

11. Do a taste test and add a little more salt and pepper, if needed.

12. Serve immediately with steamed, lighted-buttered broccoli and warm toasted garlic bread – YUM!

Green Chile Chicken Hash

6 Servings – 291 calories per serving

This a lighter version of corned-beef hash made with chicken and green chilies topped with fried or poached eggs, served with a crisp Green Salad and warm buttered French bread – perfect for dinner or Sunday Brunch.

INGREDIENTS

- 3 tablespoons butter
- 1 cup onion, finely chopped
- ¼ cup green bell pepper, finely chopped
- ½ teaspoon chili powder
- 4 cups boiled potatoes, diced
- 1 can (7 oz) Ortega® Diced Green Chiles
- 1 cup Ortega® Thick & Chunky Salsa
- 1 cup cooked chicken, cut in small cubes
- ¼ cup of vegetable oil

DIRECTIONS

1. Melt butter in a large skillet – stir in onion, bell pepper, and chili powder and cook for 5 minutes.
2. Add potatoes, chilies, salsa, and chicken; cook for 2 minutes.
3. Transfer the mixture to a medium bowl.
4. Wipe the skillet with a clean paper towel and put it back on the stove over medium heat.
5. Place the ¼ cup oil and chicken/veggie mixture in the skillet.
6. Fry over medium heat for 10 minutes or until browned.
7. Top with fried or poached eggs and serve immediately with warm buttered toast.

Linguini with Clam Sauce

4 Servings – 719 Calories per serving

This delicious pasta dish comes right out of the cupboard for a quick and easy family favorite. Add warm, fresh sourdough or French bread, a Green Salad, and the meal is complete.

INGREDIENTS

- 1 cube butter (do not use margarine)
- 2 tablespoons cooking oil
- 4 large cloves garlic, minced
- ½ teaspoon red pepper flakes – or more to taste
- ¼ cup dry white wine
- 2 cans minced clams
- Salt to taste
- Finely chopped fresh parsley
- 1 lb. linguine – cook as directed on package (use salted water)

DIRECTIONS

1. Combine oil and butter in a large heavy-duty frying pan over low heat; stir until butter is melted.
2. Add minced garlic and pepper flakes, sauté for 2 minutes.
3. Add wine and stir.
4. Add clams - including liquid.
5. Simmer over low heat for 15 minutes.
6. Cook linguini according to package instructions.
7. Drain pasta, rinse quickly with cold water to prevent sticking, drain well again, and add to clam sauce.
8. Leave the pan on the stove over low heat.

9. Toss and coat the pasta in the sauce until the pasta absorbs the flavor and juices (2 to 3 minutes).

10. Remove from heat, season with salt - place in a serving bowl.

11. Top with finely chopped parsley and Parmesan cheese and serve immediately.

New Joe's Special

6 Servings – 477 calories each

Joe's Special is an old San Francisco Italian favorite. My recipe comes from the New Joe's Restaurant in San Jose, CA. As far as I know, it is close to the original. It is perfect for brunch or a nice dinner and should be served with warm crusty sourdough bread (if you are lucky enough to find it in your area) and sweet butter.

INGREDIENTS

- 2 tablespoons olive oil
- 1½ cups chopped onion
- ½ lb. ground beef
- 2 large cloves garlic, minced
- ½ lb. mushrooms, trimmed and sliced
- 2 lbs. fresh spinach, coarsely chopped (or 1 package (10 ounces) frozen spinach, thawed and well-drained.
- 1½ teaspoons fresh oregano, minced or ½ teaspoon dried.
- Salt and freshly ground black pepper to taste
- Large dash of nutmeg, freshly grated.
- 5 large cage-free eggs, lightly beaten.
- Freshly grated parmesan cheese for topping

DIRECTIONS

1. Sauté the onion in olive oil over high heat, cook until soft, but not browned ~5 minutes.
2. Add the ground beef, garlic, and mushrooms.
3. Sauté until meat is crumbled and lightly browned - just past pink - about 10 minutes.

4. Add the spinach and cook for 5 minutes (stirring constantly).

5. Add seasoning (oregano, salt, pepper, and nutmeg to taste).

6. Reduce heat to low, add the eggs.

7. Cook and stir until eggs are just set, but still soft. Do not overcook.

8. Serve immediately - with Parmesan cheese for topping, as desired.

One-Pot Spaghetti

4 Servings – 714 Calories per serving

Spaghetti with meat sauce – a traditional favorite. This version is especially nice because it is so easy to make and cleaning up is simple. For a complete dinner, serve with Green Salad and Garlic Bread.

INGREDIENTS

- 1 tablespoon butter
- 1 medium onion, diced
- 4 cloves garlic, peeled and minced
- 1 lb. lean ground beef
- 3 cup water (or 2¾ cup water and ¼ cup red wine)
- 1 can (15 oz.) tomato sauce
- 1 small can (8 oz,) tomato paste
- 1 (15 oz.) can diced tomatoes, including juice
- 1 tablespoon Italian seasoning
- 1 teaspoon salt
- 1 teaspoon freshly ground black pepper
- ½ teaspoon sugar
- 8 to 10 oz. uncooked spaghetti
- ½ cup Parmesan cheese, freshly grated
- 2 tablespoons fresh parsley, finely chopped

DIRECTIONS

1. Place a Dutch oven (or large, heavy-duty saucepan) over medium-high heat.
2. Place 1 tablespoon butter in the pan, add chopped onion and minced garlic.
3. Sauté until onion becomes transparent and begins to brown.

111

4. Stir in the ground meat, cook until meat is browned and crumbly.

5. Spoon off any excess fat.

6. Add water, tomato sauce, tomato paste, diced tomatoes, Italian seasoning, salt, pepper, and sugar.

7. Bring meat sauce to a boil over high heat – then, break spaghetti noodles in half and drop into the sauce.

8. Reduce heat to a simmer and cover.

9. Continue cooking, stirring often to be sure noodles are separated.

10. Noodles should be cooked through in 12 to 15 minutes. Add a little water if the sauce gets too dry.

11. Stir in the parsley just before removing from heat.

12. Place grated Parmesan Cheese on the table for topping.

13. Serve while hot with Green Salad.

Creamy Pesto Chicken and Pasta

Serves 4 – 300 Calories per serving

You can prepare this dinner in 25 minutes. Serve with a green vegetable and/or green salad and your meal is ready. You can easily cut the recipe in half for just one or two servings, as you wish.

INGREDIENTS

- 1 lb. boneless, skinless chicken breasts
- Salt and freshly ground black pepper
- 2 tablespoons homemade basil pesto (or from deli section in the grocery store)
- 2 tablespoons extra virgin olive oil
- 2 cups cherry tomatoes, cut in half

For the Sauce

- 1 tablespoon flour
- 2 large garlic cloves, minced
- ½ tablespoon homemade basil pesto
- 1 cup evaporated milk
- Salt and freshly ground pepper, to taste
- Freshly grated Parmesan cheese (for garnish)
- Fresh parsley, finely chopped (for garnish)
- 8 to 10 oz pasta – whole-wheat linguini or spaghetti

DIRECTIONS

1. Bring a large pot of salted water to a boil, add the pasta, and cook according to package directions to al dente.
2. When pasta is done, drain, rinse in cold water, and mix with 1 tablespoon of olive oil to prevent sticking together; place in a warm bowl and set aside.

3. While pasta is cooking, season chicken with salt and pepper.

4. Spread fresh basil pesto over the chicken.

5. Heat olive oil in a large nonstick skillet.

6. Add chicken to the skillet and cook for 5 minutes on each side, or until thoroughly cooked.

7. While chicken is cooking, place the following in a large mixing cup: flour, garlic, basil pesto, evaporated milk, salt, and pepper.

8. Whisk ingredients until thoroughly combined; set aside.

9. Remove chicken from skillet.

10. Return skillet to heat and stir in the tomatoes. (If necessary, add a little more olive oil.)

11. Cook the tomatoes over medium-high heat for ~1 minute, or until beginning to soften.

12. Add the mixed ingredients to the skillet and bring to a boil.

13. Place the chicken back in the skillet and cook for 2 to 3 minutes, or until heated through.

14. Remove from heat.

15. Serve with pasta or Basmati brown rice.

16. Garnish with cheese and chopped parsley.

17. Serve immediately with fresh Green Salad.

Supreme Meatloaf

4 to 6 Servings - depending on appetites, with plenty left over for meatloaf sandwiches (YUM!) – 557 Calories per serving (6 Servings).

Meatloaf has always been a family favorite and wonderful comfort food. This recipe takes a little longer than some to prepare but is worth the effort. Your taste buds and your friends will thank you!

INGREDIENTS

- 2 tablespoons butter
- 1 celery stalk, very thin slices
- 1 carrot, peeled and finely chopped
- ½ cup of finely chopped green onion, including the greens
- 3 cloves garlic, minced (about 1 tablespoon)
- 2 teaspoons salt (only 1½ teaspoons if using Italian sausage)
- ½ teaspoon freshly ground black pepper
- 1 tablespoon Worcestershire sauce
- 2/3 cup catsup, divided in half
- 1½ lbs. of ground beef
- ¾ lb. of spicy ground pork sausage or Italian sausage
- 6 to 8 soda crackers, crushed
- 2 large eggs, beaten slightly
- ¼ cup whole milk (or cream)
- 1/3 cup fresh parsley, minced

DIRECTIONS

1. Preheat oven to 350° F.
2. Chop all vegetables as directed.
3. Melt the butter in a large, thick-bottomed skillet or Dutch oven over medium heat.

4. When the butter starts to bubble, add the celery, carrot, green onions, and garlic to the pan – cook for 5 minutes.

5. Cover the pan and cook for another 5 minutes, until the carrots are tender, stirring occasionally.

6. Sprinkle with salt and pepper.

7. Add the Worcestershire sauce and one-third cup of the catsup.

8. Cook for another minute and remove from heat to cool.

9. When the vegetables have cooled, place them in a large bowl with the ground beef, Italian sausage, eggs, crushed crackers, milk, and chopped parsley.

10. With VERY CLEAN hands, mix everything until well-blended.

11. Place the meatloaf mixture into a loaf pan (either 4 x 8-inch or 5 x 9-inch) and press into the pan. Or – form a free-standing loaf on a rimmed baking pan.

12. Cover the meatloaf with remaining catsup.

13. Place the meatloaf in preheated oven on a center rack and bake for about 1 hour, or until a meat thermometer inserted into the center of the meatloaf reads 165° F.

14. Remove from the oven and let rest on a wire rack for 10 minutes.

15. Gently lift the meatloaf out of the pan (a metal spatula works best).

16. Slice and serve immediately with <u>Garlic Mashed Potatoes</u> and <u>Steamed Vegetables</u>.

RECIPE NOTES
- Italian sausage is the key ingredient in this recipe! A combination of spicy and sweet is best, but if you only have one, use sweet Italian sausage.
- If Italian sausage is not available, use ground pork with ½ teaspoon of Italian Seasoning and hot sauce mixed into the meat.
- The recipe can also be made without the celery and carrots if you prefer – and is still very tasty.

White Chicken Chili

6 Servings – 383 Calories per serving/33 grams of protein

Chili is a wonderful winter meal, and this is an outstanding "remake" of traditional chili. It is hearty, creamy, and warms you to the bone. Simple to make and easy to eat. You will enjoy every bite of this yummy comfort food.

INGREDIENTS

- 1 small onion, finely diced
- 1 tablespoon olive oil
- 2 cloves garlic, minced
- 2 cans (14.5 oz.) chicken broth
- 1 can (7 oz.) diced green chilies
- 1½ teaspoon cumin
- ½ teaspoon paprika

- ½ teaspoon dried oregano
- ½ teaspoon ground coriander
- ¼ teaspoon cayenne pepper
- Salt and freshly ground black pepper, to taste
- 1 package (8 oz.) cream cheese, cut into small cubes
- 1¼ cup frozen or fresh corn
- 2 cans (15 oz.) cannellini beans
- 2 ½ cups rotisserie chicken, shredded
- 1 tablespoon fresh lime juice
- 2 tablespoons fresh cilantro, chopped (plus extra for garnish)
- 1 package tortilla chips, Monterey Jack cheese, sliced avocado - as extra toppings (optional, but tasty)

DIRECTIONS

1. Heat olive oil over medium-high heat in a 6-quart Dutch oven.
2. Add onion and sauté for 4 minutes.
3. Add garlic and sauté for 30 seconds more.
4. Add chicken broth, green chilies, cumin, paprika, oregano, coriander, and cayenne pepper.
5. Season with salt and pepper to taste.
6. Bring the mixture to a boil, then immediately reduce heat to medium-low and simmer for 15 minutes.
7. Drain beans in a colander or fine mesh strainer and measure out 1 cup of beans; set remaining beans aside.
8. Place the cup of beans in a blender with ¼ cup broth from the soup and purée until smooth. *(Be careful when blending hot foods, they can explode and burn you.)*
9. Add cream cheese cubes, corn, whole beans, and bean puree to the soup.
10. Stir well and simmer for 5 to 10 minutes more.
11. Stir in the shredded chicken, fresh lime juice, and cilantro.

12. Serve in large soup bowls with Monterey Jack cheese, more chopped cilantro, avocado slices, and tortilla chips as toppings

RECIPE NOTES

- If you don't have a blender or food processor to purée the beans, you can mash them by hand or just skip that step. It will not be as creamy, but it will still be delicious.

DINNERS TO IMPRESS

The dishes in this section are a bit more complicated but should be part of your repertoire. There will be occasions when you want to serve an out-of-the-ordinary dinner to special guests or for a celebratory feast.

The four entrées I have included are at the top of my list when preparing a dinner to impress. All four are made with chicken, which is one of the more economical meats.

The recipes may be challenging the first time you prepare them, so don't rush. Take your time and follow the recipes to the letter. Each time you prepare them, the process will be easier.

I have also included my *Thanksgiving Turkey and Dressing* recipe, which has been in my family for 50+ years. Anyone who has eaten my dressing will tell you it is the best! Now, it can be yours to pass down through the generations.

Chicken Divan

6 Servings – 711 Calories per serving

This is an excellent choice for special occasions, or to quietly demonstrate your culinary skills to important guests. It requires several steps to prepare, but the outcome is worth the time and energy. Prepare, serve, and enjoy the accolades.

INGREDIENTS

- 2 cups medium white sauce *(Prepare first – make with half chicken stock and half milk)*
- 2 lbs. fresh broccoli spears
- 3 lbs. chicken breast halves, boneless and skinless
- 1 teaspoon salt
- 1 medium onion, quartered
- 2 cups of water

- 2 stalks celery with leaves, cut in large chunks
- ½ cup Hollandaise Sauce *(Recipe below – Aunt Penny's canned sauce is an acceptable substitute.)*
- ½ teaspoon salt
- 1½ teaspoon Worcestershire sauce
- 4½ tablespoons sherry
- ¾ cup whipping cream
- 1½ cups grated parmesan cheese
- 6 to 8 fresh mushrooms, washed and sliced

DIRECTIONS

1. Prepare homemade white sauce (recipe below) and Hollandaise sauce (recipe below) – or use Aunt Penny's Canned Sauces for both. *(Freshly made is better.)*
2. Simmer chicken in water with salt, celery stalks/leaves, and onion, until chicken is tender ~about 25 minutes.
3. Separate broccoli into flowerets and steam until barely fork tender – DO NOT OVERCOOK.
4. Make the Hollandaise sauce.
5. Combine the white sauce with the Hollandaise sauce; add salt, sherry, and Worcestershire sauce.
6. Butter a large casserole baking dish and arrange broccoli around the edge of the dish, place the remainder evenly in the center of the dish.
7. Add a layer of sliced mushrooms.
8. Sprinkle with half of the cheese.
9. Arrange sliced chicken on top.
10. Whip cream until stiff and fold gently into the combined sauces.
11. Spoon over the chicken.
12. Top with remaining cheese.

13. Bake in a hot oven - 400° F. for 20 minutes. *(Be careful not to overcook or the sauce will separate.)*
14. Place about 5 inches under the broiler and broil until top is lightly browned and bubbly.
15. Serve at once with hot French bread, sweet butter, and a crisp Green Salad.

RECIPE NOTES

- Frozen broccoli and canned mushroom pieces can be used, if necessary, although the dish is much better with fresh vegetables.

White Sauce

White sauce, also known as Béchamel, is used in a variety of dishes and is the base for many sauces. Here are the steps for a basic medium white sauce, with adjustments for thickness. It is the perfect base for chicken casserole dishes and the wonderful comfort food, macaroni and cheese.

INGREDIENTS

- 4 tablespoons butter (DO NOT use margarine)
- 4 tablespoons flour
- 2 cups whole milk
- ¼ teaspoon salt
- 1 dash white pepper
- 1 dash grated or ground nutmeg

DIRECTIONS

1. Place a heavy saucepan over medium-low heat, melt the butter.
2. Stir the flour into the melted butter with a wire whisk – continue whisking until well blended and smooth.
3. Cook over low heat for 3 minutes while the mixture begins to bubble.
4. Stir constantly - do not allow the mixture to brown. This mixture is called a roux.
5. Remove the pan from the heat and whisk in the milk.
6. Return pan to heat and bring to a simmer, stirring continuously.
7. Continue cooking and whisking until sauce is thick and smooth – approximately 2 to 3 minutes.
8. Add the dash of nutmeg and season to taste with salt and pepper.

Easy Hollandaise Sauce

Hollandaise Sauce has always been daunting, but anyone can make it with this recipe and enjoy the results. Spread it generously over fish, steamed broccoli or asparagus, or on top of poached eggs, bacon, and English muffins. Eggs Benedict, anyone?

INGREDIENTS

- ½ cup unsalted butter (DO NOT use margarine)
- 3 large cage-free egg yolks
- 1 tablespoon lemon juice
- 1 tablespoon sherry
- 3 dashes cayenne pepper
- ½ teaspoon salt (if using salted butter, omit the salt)

DIRECTIONS

1. Melt the butter in a small saucepan.
2. Remove from heat as soon as it is melted. Do not let it sizzle.
3. Place the egg yolks, lemon juice, sherry, salt, and cayenne in an electric blender and blend on medium speed for 20 to 30 seconds or until the mixture lightens in color.
4. When color changes, reduce the speed to the lowest setting and very slowly add the melted butter – continue to blend for 3 or 4 seconds after all the butter has been added.
5. Taste the sauce – it should taste buttery, lemony, and very lightly salted. If necessary, add the necessary ingredients (salt or lemon) to enhance the flavor.
6. If you want the sauce thinner, add a little warm water and pulse two or three short pulses to thoroughly mix the additional ingredients.
7. Either serve immediately or keep the sauce in a warm place (on the stovetop) and serve within an hour.

Chicken Jerusalem

6 Servings – 370 Calories per serving

The first time I enjoyed this amazing dish was at Ernie's Restaurant in San Francisco when I was 24 years old. It was the most delicious meal I had ever eaten. I finally got the recipe! The white wine and butter sauce give the chicken an exquisite finish.

INGREDIENTS

- 6 chicken breast halves, boneless, skinless
- ½ cup butter
- 2 green onions, chopped
- ½ cup white wine
- ½ cup of water
- 1 cup fresh mushrooms, sliced
- 2 teaspoons salt

- 2 cans (14 oz) artichoke hearts
- Parmesan cheese
- Parsley, chopped for garnish
- Green onions, chopped for garnish

DIRECTIONS

1. In a large skillet, melt butter and brown chicken pieces.
2. Add green onions, water, and wine - simmer for 45 minutes.
3. Add the mushrooms, salt, and artichoke hearts - simmer for an additional 15 minutes.
4. Before serving, top with grated parmesan cheese.
5. Garnish lightly with green onions and parsley.
6. Serve with wild/white rice pilaf and steamed broccoli.

RECIPE NOTES

- To make the dish richer, use chicken broth instead of water; and sauté 2 cloves of garlic in the butter before adding to the chicken.

Chicken Scaloppini
with Lemon Garlic Cream Sauce

4 Servings – 228 Calories per serving

This is traditional chicken scaloppini with a delightful flavor twist. The lemon garlic cream sauce is a touch of heavenly delight. You will want to prepare this dish often. This is the easiest of the four chicken dishes in this section.

INGREDIENTS
The Chicken

- 2 large whole chicken breasts, boneless, skinless, and cut in half to make 4 fillets
- 2 lemons, cut in half (using juice only)
- 1 teaspoon garlic powder
- 1 teaspoon salt
- Freshly ground pepper
- 4 tablespoons flour

The Sauce
- 1 tablespoon butter
- 2 teaspoons oil
- 1 medium onion
- 6 to 8 cloves garlic, minced (2 tablespoons)
- 1¼ cup chicken broth or stock
- 2/3 cup heavy cream (can also use half-and-half)
- 1 teaspoon cornstarch mixed with 1 tablespoon of water
- 3 tablespoons lemon juice, adjust to taste
- 2 teaspoons dried Italian mixed herbs *(substitute 1½ teaspoons dried basil and ½ teaspoon dried oregano)*
- 2 tablespoons fresh parsley, chopped (for garnish)
- Lemon slices or wedges (for garnish)

DIRECTIONS
1. Squeeze the lemon juice of half a lemon over each fillet, rubbing it into each chicken fillet.
2. Season with garlic powder, salt, and pepper.
3. Put the flour in a shallow bowl and dredge each fillet in the flour.
4. Shake off excess and set aside.
5. Heat the butter and oil in a large skillet or non-stick pan over medium-high heat until the butter has melted, and the pan is hot.
6. Fry the chicken until golden on each side and no longer pink in the center ~ 4-5 minutes per side.
7. Transfer onto a warm plate.
8. Add the onion and garlic to the pan and sauté until onion is translucent ~3 minutes.
9. Reduce heat to low-medium heat, add the broth.
10. Season with salt and pepper.
11. Continue to cook for about 6 minutes to reduce the liquid.

12. Add the cream and bring the sauce to a gentle simmer for about 5 minutes until it begins to thicken.

13. If the sauce is too thin, quickly pour in the cornstarch/water into the mixture and stir briskly to combine. It will begin to thicken immediately.

14. Add the lemon juice, allow to simmer gently for a minute more.

15. Stir in the Italian herbs.

16. Add the chicken back into the pan, cover with the sauce.

17. Serve over rice or pasta with a side of steamed vegetables.

18. Garnish with lemon slices and chopped parsley.

Coq au Vin

6 Servings - 776 Calories per serving

Coq au Vin is a classic French dish with a rich, red wine sauce. It is a surprisingly easy way to make mouth-watering chicken (although it does take some time and effort). This is one of those recipes that is more fun if there are two of you in the kitchen. Serve with a crusty baguette for dunking the seriously delicious sauce. This is the most challenging recipe in the book, but if you take your time, it will be amazing.

INGREDIENTS

Marinate the Chicken

- 4 lbs. chicken thigh and drumsticks, skin removed
- 12 ounces red wine (Chianti is a good choice)
- ¼ cup Cognac or good brandy
- 4 large cloves garlic, crushed
- 2 sprigs fresh thyme

- 1 whole bay leaves
- 3 to 4 pieces fresh parsley, chopped including stems

Brown the Chicken
- Kosher salt and pepper to season chicken
- ¼ cup olive oil

Make the Stew
- 1 medium-large Vidalia onion, chopped
- 1 whole carrot, chopped
- 2 stalks celery, chopped
- 2 tablespoon tomato paste
- 3 tablespoons flour
- 1½ teaspoon salt
- ½ teaspoon pepper
- 1 cup chicken stock

Finishing Touches
- 1/3 lb. good bacon or pancetta, diced
- ½ lb. button mushrooms, stems removed and sliced thick
- 1 lb. noodles, cooked al dente according to packaged instructions
- 3 tablespoons butter

DIRECTIONS

Marinate the chicken the night before

1. Remove skin and excess fat from the chicken pieces, wash under cold running water, and pat dry with paper towels.
2. Place the chicken a large bowl, and cover with a mixture of wine, brandy, garlic, thyme, bay leaf, and whole parsley stems.

3. Cover and marinate for 24 hours in the refrigerator.

4. Remove chicken from marinade and pat dry, reserving marinade.

Brown the chicken

5. In a large Dutch oven, cook chicken on all sides in 2 tablespoons oil over medium heat until golden brown (5 – 7 minutes).

6. Season the chicken with salt and pepper while cooking.

7. Remove chicken to a plate.

Make the stew

8. In the same pot, add more oil if needed and sauté the onions, carrot, and celery until tender.

9. Add, salt, pepper, and tomato paste - cook until the mixture turns a deep reddish-brown color (will be very thick and you may need to add ½ cup water.

10. Add flour and stir until thoroughly mixed and begins to bubble, then pour in the reserved marinade – stirring continuously with a wire whisk.

11. Continue to stir and simmer until thickened ~10 minutes.

12. Add chicken back to the pot with the sauce and pour in enough chicken stock to just come up the sides of the chicken but not cover it completely.

13. Bring to a boil - then, cover, lower to a simmer, and cook for about 1 hour or until the chicken falls off the bone.

14. Gently remove chicken from pot and strain the liquid from the solids, discarding the solids.

15. Return chicken and strained liquid to the Dutch oven and bring to a simmer.

Cook the noodles

1. Cook the noodles according to package directions.

Put it all together

1. Heat a large sauté pan with remaining 2 tablespoons oil over medium-high heat.
2. Add bacon (pancetta) to the pan and cook until crispy then add mushrooms.
3. Reduce heat and sauté until mushrooms are tender and browned.
4. Add the mixture into the pot with the chicken and sauce.
5. Toss the noodles with butter.
6. Place the noodles on a serving platter or individual plates and top with the chicken and sauce.
7. Garnish with chopped parsley and serve.

RECIPE NOTES

- It can be served over rice or mashed potatoes, or plain with warm fresh, crusty French bread to soak up the amazing sauce.

Thanksgiving Turkey and Dressing

6 Servings – (Calories - Who cares??? It's the Holidays!)

This recipe can be used for roast chicken or turkey. It turns out a lovely, moist, delicious bird with a tasty stuffing and gravy. The recipe has been in my family for years - and still considered "the best dressing in the world" by my children no matter how many other turkey and dressing dinners they try.

INGREDIENTS

Turkey

- 1 whole turkey, fresh or frozen (12 to 16 lbs.)

Dressing

- ½ to ¾ lb. mild to medium sausage
- 8 tablespoons butter (1 cube) DO NOT use margarine
- 1½ cups celery, very finely sliced
- 3 smalls to medium onions, finely chopped

137

- 2 medium green apples, cored, peeled, and finely chopped *(Personal preference is Granny Smith apples)*
- 1 large carrot, peeled, split vertically, and sliced very thinly
- 1 clove garlic (large), minced
- 1 can water chestnuts, drained and sliced very thinly
- Salt and pepper for vegetables *(use a light hand at this point)*
- 2 packages (8 oz) Pepperidge Farms® Cornbread Stuffing Mix *(Use 3 packages for a larger bird)*
- 1 teaspoon salt
- ½ teaspoon black pepper
- 3 tablespoons fresh parsley, coarsely chopped *(Remove stems, rinse, and let dry before chopped)*
- 1 teaspoon dried thyme leaves
- 1 teaspoon ground sage
- ½ teaspoon dried oregano

To Moisten Dressing
- ½ cup half-and-half
- ½ cup chicken broth *(use remaining for basting mixture)*
- 1 can water chestnuts, drained
- 2 large cage-free eggs
- ½ cup sherry
- 1 tablespoon lemon juice

Basting Mixture
- Remaining chicken broth from the can
- ¼ cup sherry
- ¼ cup butter *(not margarine)*

Extra
- Aluminum foil - to cover the turkey

Gravy

- Chicken giblets
- Water to cover giblets
- 1 medium onion, peeled and quartered
- 4 stalks celery (tops only)
- 1 large carrot, peeled and quartered
- Salt and pepper to taste
- 1 teaspoon poultry seasoning
- 3 to 4 tablespoons flour (or cornstarch)
- Hot water –to thin gravy, if necessary

DIRECTIONS

1. NEVER stuff a turkey until you are ready to cook it!
2. This recipe is for 12 to 16 lb. turkey. My recommendation is a 12-lb. turkey. Fresh or frozen (thawed) – my personal choice is a Butterball Turkey.

The Gravy – Step One

3. Remove giblets from turkey and place in a large saucepan, cover with water.
4. Return turkey to the refrigerator until ready to stuff.
5. Add a medium onion, peeled and cut into wedges, tops of celery stalks, a peeled and chopped carrot, poultry seasoning, plus salt and pepper.
6. Simmer on low heat for approximately 60 minutes - remove from heat, set aside, and use later for the gravy.

Prepare the Dressing

1. Prepare the vegetables *(peel, chop, and slice).*
2. Fry the sausage until crumbled into small pieces and lightly browned - not burned or crispy. Drain fat and set aside to cool.

3.   Melt 1 cube of butter in large, heavy frying pan over medium-high heat.

4.   Add ingredients to the hot butter in the order listed: celery, onions, apples, carrot, garlic, sliced water chestnuts (1 can), salt and pepper to taste.

5.   Cook until onions and celery are soft and turning transparent.

6.   While vegetables are cooking, place cornbread stuffing mix into an extra-large mixing bowl.

7.   Add the seasonings: salt, pepper, parsley, thyme, sage, and oregano.

8.   Add sausage and cooked vegetables *(including butter juices in the pan)*.

9.   In an electric blender, mix the following until smooth: half-and-half, chicken broth, 1 can water chestnuts (drained), eggs, sherry, and lemon juice.

10.   Pour liquid mixture over the dressing ingredients and stir well – dressing should be moist and hold together slightly.

NOTE: Use only as much of the liquid as needed to moisten dressing well - better for the dressing to be a little dry than too moist. If you need more liquid than what you have prepared, use additional sherry or chicken broth.

Stuff the Turkey

11.   Heat oven to 325° F.

12.   Wash the turkey quickly under cold running water.

13.   Dry thoroughly inside and out with clean, dry paper towels.

14.   Lightly salt the inside of both cavities.

15.   Fill wishbone area (neck cavity) with stuffing – do not pack tightly.

16.   To cover the cavity, fasten neck skin to back with skewer.

17.   Fold wings across the back with tips touching.

18. Fill body cavity - do not hard pack - dressing will expand while cooking.

19. Tuck drumsticks under band of skin at tail and skewer skin together - or tie drumsticks together with heavy string, then tie to tail.

20. Place in a large roasting pan - breast side down.

21. Rub the turkey with softened butter, pour a generous amount of sherry over the turkey and sprinkle lightly with garlic salt.

22. Bake for 1½ to 2 hours, then lower heat to 300° F.

23. Baste every 30 minutes with a basting mixture of melted butter and sherry.

24. Leave the breast down until the bottom of turkey is brown; then turn breast side up.

25. After turning - Insert meat thermometer with the tip inside the thickest part of breast meat - must not touch any bone.

26. Roast uncovered until the breast is lightly browned, then cover browned areas loosely with foil. Watch the legs, they brown easily.

27. A 12- to 16-lb. turkey (completely thawed) will take 4½ to 5½ hours to cook. The internal temperature on a meat thermometer must be 185 degrees.

28. When the turkey is 2/3 done, cut band of skin or the string holding legs.

29. When the turkey is done, transfer to a large platter, cover with foil, and let it rest for 20 minutes to make carving easier.

Make the Gravy

1. If you wish to make giblet gravy, strain the giblets and vegetables from the saucepan, reserving liquid.

2. Chop the giblets and pick any meat off neck bones, place meat in a blender and add the liquid.

3. Blend until liquid and smooth, add 3 or 4 tablespoons flour or corn starch and blend again to mix well.

4. Pour off as much fat as possible from the roasting pan.
5. With a wooden spoon, scrape any bits and pieces of stuffing/chicken stuck to the bottom, remove any large pieces of skin.
6. Add the giblet mix from the blender, whisk around until thoroughly mixed.
7. Place in 450° F. to 500° F. oven until the mixture is bubbly ~10 minutes.
8. If gravy is too thick, add water slowly, stirring constantly, until it reaches desired consistency. *(We like our gravy medium thick.)*
9. Cook another 5 minutes.
10. Salt and pepper to taste.
11. Whisk and pour into a gravy boat.
12. Serve hot with the roasted turkey, dressing, and mashed potatoes.
13. Serve with all the trimmings and ENJOY every bite!!

NOTE: *Gravy can also be made without the giblets, just whisk up the brown bits in the roaster and add 1 cup of hot water and make a slurry of cold water and either flour or corn starch, add the slurry and whisk, cook the same as above, adding a little more water if necessary.*

RECIPE NOTES
- *A meat thermometer* is recommended, but you can also test for doneness by moving the drumstick up and down. If it is done, the joint should move easily or break.
- Or - press drumstick meat between fingers - the meat should be very soft.
- Extra dressing can be cooked separately in a 9 X 13-inch baking dish at 350° F. for 30 minutes.

USING THE LEFTOVERS

- As soon as possible after dinner, remove EVERY bit of stuffing from turkey.
- Stuffing, meat, and any remaining gravy should no longer be hot; refrigerate separately!
- Use remaining gravy and stuffing within 1 or 2 days - heat thoroughly before serving.
- Turkey can be eaten for 2 or 3 days after roasting. Frozen, it will keep up to a month.
- Suggestions for leftover turkey: Turkey Soup, Turkey and Dressing Casserole, Turkey Sandwiches *(Use fresh bread or rolls; plenty of good mayo, sliced turkey, dressing, cranberry sauce)*.

Side Dishes

Many entrées can be served without a side dish because they are a complete meal by themselves. Other entrées will need side dishes to provide all the essential nutrients for good health and to complete the meal.

We recommend that you start with the easiest choices: Baked Potatoes, Steamed Vegetables, and Green Salad. Once you have mastered those, you can move on to some of the others that take a little more time but add extra appeal to your presentation.

We have included several side dishes made from healthy carbohydrates – potatoes, pasta, and rice; plus, several easy vegetable dishes - dressed up to make them more appealing for those who do not relish the idea of eating their vegetables.

Note on the carbohydrates: Always use whole-wheat pasta and Basmati brown rice, if possible. They are much healthier than white pasta and rice.

Some will become immediate favorites, but I encourage you to change it up often and eventually try them all. You may be surprised which ones you like best.

Asparagus Risotto

6 Servings – 159 Calories per serving

This is an excellent side dish to accompany any entrée, especially good with roasted chicken or grilled steak.

INGREDIENTS

- 1 lb. fresh asparagus
- 1 teaspoon salt
- 1 cup onions, chopped
- 1 large garlic clove, minced
- 1 tablespoon vegetable oil or olive oil
- 1 tablespoon butter
- 1 cup raw medium-grained rice *(use Arborio rice, if available)*
- ¼ cup fresh parsley, chopped
- 1/3 cup Romano or Parmesan cheese, grated
- Salt and freshly ground pepper, to taste

DIRECTIONS

1. Wash asparagus and break off ends by bending and going with the natural break.
2. Cook in a vegetable steamer or boil in salted water in a large saucepan ~12 minutes and drain.
3. Reserve cooking liquid and add enough water to reach 5 cups of liquid; set aside.
4. Heat butter and oil in a large skillet over medium-high heat.
5. Add onion and garlic; cook until onion is limp and garlic slightly browned.
6. Add rice; stir 2 to 3 minutes until well coated and beginning to turn opaque.
7. Stir in 1 cup reserved asparagus liquid.
8. Cook, uncovered, stirring frequently until liquid is absorbed.
9. Continue stirring as you add the remaining asparagus liquid - 1 cup at a time (total of 5 cups), allowing each cup to be absorbed before adding another.
10. Rice should be tender, and the mixture should have a creamy consistency - it will take approximately 25 to 30 minutes.
11. Stir in asparagus, parsley, cheese, and salt, if desired.

RECIPE NOTES

- Use crisp, fresh asparagus.
- You can serve the risotto exactly as prepared above or be creative.
- Change-up the dish by adding lemon zest, lump crab meat, and green onion. Then, garnish with thyme or chopped mint.

Asparagus with Lemon and Parmesan

4 Servings – 88 Calories per serving

Slightly crunchy, bright-green asparagus with a hint of lemon flavor, combined with the olive oil and Parmesan cheese makes this a delicious, colorful accompaniment to almost any entrée.

INGREDIENTS

- 1 lb. asparagus spears, medium-sized
- 2 tablespoons extra-virgin olive oil – high grade, PLEASE
- 2 tablespoons Parmesan cheese, freshly grated preferred
- 1 teaspoon lemon zest (freshly grated lemon rind)
- Salt and freshly ground black pepper, to taste

DIRECTIONS

1. Prepare the asparagus by rinsing thoroughly, popping off the ends where they break naturally.
2. Cut on a diagonal into 2-inch pieces.
3. Place the olive oil, parmesan cheese, and lemon rind in a bowl.
4. Fill a medium-sized saucepan half full and bring to a boil.
5. Add the asparagus and reduce heat to a simmer.
6. Parboil the asparagus for exactly 2 minutes and drain off the water. DO NOT OVERCOOK! Mushy asparagus will ruin this dish.
7. Immediately place the hot asparagus into the bowl with the olive oil, parmesan cheese, and lemon rind.
8. Gently toss until all pieces are well-covered.
9. Salt and pepper, to taste.
10. Serve warm or at room temperature.

RECIPE NOTES

- When you are working with so few ingredients, you must use only the best ingredients you can find.
- Broccoli is a nice substitute for this dish.

Best Baked Potatoes

4 Servings – 290 Calories per serving (without butter or toppings)

Potatoes, potatoes, potatoes. They often take a bad rap, but wrongfully so. They are loaded with vitamins, minerals, potassium, and antioxidants. They are extremely versatile – as you will see by all the recipes we have included – **and they are good for you***.*

INGREDIENTS

- 4 russet potatoes (about 2½ lbs.), well-scrubbed
- Olive oil (for rubbing)
- Flaky sea salt
- Freshly ground black pepper
- Unsalted butter

For Toppings

- Finely grated Parmesan (or your favorite cheese)
- Chopped fresh chives
- Spice it up with Indian Flavors like the exotic spice blend: chat masala.
- Favorites (Everything should be finely chopped)
  - Chutney
  - Green chilies
  - Red onions
  - Ginger
  - Cilantro
  - Sour cream

DIRECTIONS

1. Preheat the oven to 375° F.

2. Scrubbed each potato carefully – do not remove the skin.

3. Rub each potato with olive oil.

4. Cook until fork slides in and out of the center easily (about 45 minutes).

5. Serve as a side dish for dinner with butter, sea salt, and pepper.

6. Allow individuals to add their favorite toppings.

7. Very small potatoes can be cut with a crosshatch, topped with a variety of toppings, and served as appetizers.

Buttered Pasta

8 Servings – 108 Calories per serving

This is a quick and easy way to serve pasta, which goes with almost any main course. It is a nice change from potatoes and rice.

INGREDIENTS

- 2 quarts chicken stock
- 8 ounces dry pasta (noodles, spaghetti, fettuccine, etc. – your choice)
- 1 teaspoon salt
- 2 tablespoons butter
- 2 large cloves garlic, minced
- 2 tablespoons fresh parsley, finely chopped
- Salt and freshly ground black pepper, to taste
- Grated parmesan cheese (optional)

DIRECTIONS

1. Bring stock to a boil in a large pot and add salt.
2. Add pasta and cook until tender but firm to the bite (al dente) ~ 8 minutes.
3. While pasta is cooking, melt butter in a small saucepan and stir in garlic and parsley - heat gently.
4. Drain cooked pasta, thoroughly and place on a heated platter.
5. Pour butter mixture over pasta and toss to coat well.
6. Serve hot with parmesan cheese as an optional topping.

RECIPE NOTES

- Cut butter amount slightly and eliminate the parsley.
- Top with a large dollop of good basil pesto before serving. Adds color and flavor.

Broccoli with Lemon Mustard Sauce

6 Servings – 123 Calories per serving (with sauce)

My favorite is steamed broccoli served lightly buttered with salt and pepper, but occasionally it is fun to dress it up. This easy recipe works best with the tops (florets), which my granddaughter calls the trees. Save the stalks - peel, slice, and eat raw with a dip - a great snack food, with very few calories.

INGREDIENTS

The Broccoli

- 1 tablespoon high-quality extra-virgin olive oil
- 1 teaspoon garlic, fresh and finely chopped
- 3 cups broccoli florets (about 2 lbs.)
- Freshly ground black pepper
- Juice of 1 whole lemon

The Sauce (Optional)

- ½ cup real mayonnaise – Best Foods® or Hellman's®
- 3 tablespoons Dijon mustard
- 2 tablespoons fresh lemon juice

DIRECTIONS

Cook the Broccoli

1. Heat oil in heavy skillet or wok.
2. Add garlic and cook for 30 seconds.
3. Add broccoli and toss until tender, but crisp (about 7 minutes).
4. With a slotted spoon, transfer broccoli to a heated bowl.
5. Sprinkle with pepper and lemon juice.
6. Serve immediately, as is, or top each serving with Mock Hollandaise Sauce (below).

The Sauce (Optional)

1. Mix mayonnaise, mustard, and lemon juice in a small bowl.
2. Blend with wire whisk until smooth and creamy.
3. Makes about 1 cup.

Cauliflower with
Garlic Lemon Butter Sauce

6 Servings – 91 Calories per serving

*When prepared well, cauliflower is a very tasty side dish. I think you will enjoy this easy recipe. Also, try topping it with **Creamy Cheese Sauce** (recipe follows this one and shown in picture).*

INGREDIENTS

- 1 medium head cauliflower
- 1½ cups milk
- 2 tablespoons butter
- 2 large cloves garlic, finely minced
- 2 tablespoons fresh parsley, finely chopped
- 2 teaspoons lemon juice, freshly squeezed

DIRECTIONS

1. Remove leaves and stalks - cut cauliflower head from the stem.
2. Cut or break apart into large florets and place them in a saucepan.
3. Add 1½ cups milk to the pan and bring to a boil.
4. Reduce heat, cover partially, and simmer until the cauliflower is just barely tender ~10 to 20 minutes. Check often - DO NOT overcook.
5. Melt butter in a small saucepan.
6. Add garlic, parsley, and lemon juice; mix well.
7. When cauliflower is done, drain and place in a warm serving dish.
8. Pour butter mixture over cauliflower (or top with the cheese sauce below.)
9. Serve immediately.

Cheese Sauce for Vegetables

5 (¼ cup) Servings – 260 Calories per serving

This a wonderful sauce to dress up vegetables. It is perfect for a medley of steamed vegetables, a combination of cauliflower and peas, or a single dish such as broccoli. It also adds a nice touch to chicken. It can be mixed in or served on the side.

INGREDIENTS

- ½ cup butter (1 cube)
- 3 tablespoons flour
- ½ tablespoon prepared mustard
- 1½ cups milk
- 8 ounces grated cheddar cheese
- ½ teaspoon salt
- Dash Cayenne pepper
- Dash paprika

- 1 tablespoon crushed finely chopped onions
- 1 tablespoon Worcestershire sauce

DIRECTIONS

1. Blend butter, flour, and mustard in a saucepan.
2. Add milk and place over low heat, stirring constantly until heated through.
3. Add grated cheese and all seasonings.
4. The mixture will begin to thicken gradually.
5. When it reaches the desired consistency, remove from the heat.
6. Serve warm with chicken or on almost any vegetable or combination of vegetables.

Creamed Spinach

6 Servings – 152 Calories per serving

This is a rich version of traditional creamed spinach that goes well with steamed basmati rice, cold sliced tomatoes, and grilled or baked chicken or fish.

INGREDIENTS

- 2 lbs. fresh spinach, washed, chopped, and steamed
- 1 tablespoon garlic, minced
- 2 tablespoons butter
- 1 tablespoon flour
- 1 cup half-and-half
- 2 tablespoons Parmesan cheese, grated
- 1/8 teaspoon nutmeg
- ½ teaspoon salt
- 1/8 teaspoon pepper

DIRECTIONS

1. Wash fresh spinach thoroughly, shake the water from leaves and dry off excess water with paper towels.

2. Chop spinach and steam in a vegetable steamer until barely limp. *(Do not overcook.)*

3. Remove container with spinach from the steamer to stop cooking.

4. Gently press with a paper towel to remove excess moisture; set aside.

5. Melt butter in a medium-sized saucepan over medium heat.

6. Sauté minced garlic in butter for 1 minute.

7. Whisk flour into melted butter, stirring constantly for another minute.

8. Continue to whisk and add half-and-half, cheese, nutmeg, salt, and pepper; bring to a light simmer.

9. Add spinach to the creamy cheese sauce and simmer on low for 10 minutes.

10. Serve immediately with extra parmesan for topping.

Fresh Corn Sauté

6 Servings – 195 Calories per serving

This is a great way to serve fresh corn. Even the children will eat it without a problem. It is SOOOOO good!

INGREDIENTS

- 3 tablespoons butter
- ½ cup onion, finely diced
- ½ small green pepper, trimmed, seeded, and finely diced
- 1 small zucchini, trimmed, scraped, and finely diced
- 5 to 6 ears fresh corn – parboiled and kernels cut from the cob
- ¼ cup water
- 1 tablespoon honey
- 1 teaspoon salt
- 1/8 teaspoon freshly ground black pepper
- 2 tablespoons fresh parsley, very finely chopped
- ½ cup cheddar cheese, grated (optional)

DIRECTIONS

1. Shuck and parboil corn-on-the-cob for 2 or 3 minutes in boiling water.
2. Cool under running cold water and cut kernels from the cobs.
3. Place in a bowl and set aside.
4. Melt butter in a medium skillet with a cover.
5. Sauté onions and green pepper until tender.
6. Add corn, zucchini, water, honey, seasonings, and parsley.
7. Cover and cook over low heat stirring several times until corn is crisp-tender.
8. Serve hot topped with cheese (optional).

RECIPE NOTES

- Add a little finely chopped cilantro for a mild Southwestern flavor.
- Use cooked, crumbled bacon as an additional topping with the cheese.

Fried Potatoes and Onions

4 Servings – 174 calories per serving

This is a comfort food dish that my mother served often, probably because potatoes were a staple in our home, and it is so easy to prepare. I don't think it is served as often as it once was, but it should be revived. It was served both as a side dish for dinner and as a main dish for breakfast with ham or bacon.

INGREDIENTS

- 2 tablespoons bacon fat *(preferred, but can use a combination of butter and olive oil)*
- 6 medium potatoes, thinly sliced
- ½ large Vidalia onion, sliced thinly or chopped finely.
- ¼ green pepper, chopped (optional)
- Salt and pepper, to taste
- Additional butter, as needed

- Additional seasonings, as desired: seasoning salt, Cajun/Creole seasoning, garlic salt or powder.

DIRECTIONS

1. Wash and peel potatoes; pat dry and cut into very thin slices.
2. Heat bacon grease *(or butter/oil combination in a cast-iron skillet or very heavy frying pan)*.
3. Add the potatoes, onion, and bell pepper all at once.
4. Turn the heat up medium-high and sprinkle with salt and pepper.
5. Stir to make sure seasonings are mixed in well and the vegetables are coated with the oil.
6. Cook uncovered, without turning. This will allow the bottom layer to brown.
7. Then, stir occasionally to turn and cook all sides of the potatoes.
8. Continue frying uncovered, stirring occasionally until the potatoes are tender and you reach the desired level of browning.
9. Adjust the heat and add additional butter, as needed.
10. Taste test and adjust seasonings, as needed.
11. Add additional seasonings that you like, such as garlic salt or Cajun spices.
12. Serve immediately.

RECIPE NOTES

- Use a cast-iron skillet for this dish for best results. If you do not have one, it is a good investment.
- We usually sliced our potatoes and onions as described in the recipe; but, some people like them cubed which allows them to cook a little differently. You may want to try it both ways - cubed and sliced – see which you prefer.

- Any type of potato will work. Try different types and see which you prefer.
- Some people also add sweet bell pepper, but the dish is certainly just as good without them.
- Fried Potatoes and Onions can also be used as a side dish for supper, stir in a few fresh chopped herbs just before serving. Good choices would be crushed or chopped rosemary, chopped dill, thyme, oregano, or flat-leaf (Italian) parsley.
- Red-skinned potatoes are particularly good as a supper side dish.

Garlic Bread

This wonderful garlic bread can be made two different ways – grilled crispy under the boiler (as shown below) or soft and buttery from being wrapped in foil and heated in the oven (picture on the following page). Try it both ways and find out which you prefer.

Toasted Deliciousness from the Broiler

INGREDIENTS

- A 16-ounce loaf of French bread
- ½ cup (1 stick) unsalted butter, softened
- 1 teaspoon garlic salt
- 1 heaping tablespoon of finely chopped fresh parsley (optional)
- ¼ cup freshly grated Parmesan cheese (optional)

DIRECTIONS

1. Preheat oven to 350° F.
2. Line a heavy-duty cookie sheet with foil.
3. Mix the butter, garlic salt, and parsley in a small bowl.
4. Cut the loaf of bread in half, lengthwise.
5. Spread a generous amount of the butter mixture over both halves of the bread.
6. Place the bread on the foil-lined cookie sheet and put in the preheated oven on the middle rack.
7. Let it heat in the oven for 10 minutes.
8. If you are using Parmesan, remove from the oven and sprinkle with the cheese *(if not using cheese, skip to the next step).*
9. Move the cookie sheet to the highest rack and change the oven to "BROIL"
10. Broil for 2-3 minutes until the edges of the bread are toasted and the cheese bubbles *(if you are using cheese).*
11. Watch very carefully while broiling. The bread can quickly go from un-toasted to burnt.
12. Remove from the oven and let the bread cool a minute.
13. Cut the halves into 1-inch slices.
14. Serve immediately.

Soft and Buttery from the Oven

DIRECTIONS

1. Preheat oven to 350° F.
2. Make the butter/garlic/parsley mixture as described above.
3. Cut 1-inch thick slices through the loaf of bread, but do not cut all the way through, cut almost to the bottom crust.
4. Put a teaspoon of the butter mixture between every other slice so that it is only buttered on one side of each slice.
5. If you like super buttery bread put a teaspoon of butter mixture between every slice.
6. Wrap the bread in aluminum foil and heat for 15 minutes in the preheated oven.
7. Cool a little, then, cut each slice completely through and place in a covered breadbasket.

Garlic Mashed Potatoes

6 Servings – 351 Calories per serving

Mashed potatoes are very traditional and loved by most people. The recipe can be made with or without garlic and cheese. Either way, it is a versatile side dish for almost any entrée.

INGREDIENTS

- 2 lbs. potatoes
- 1 tablespoons salt
- ½ cube butter (not margarine)
- ¾ cup half-and-half
- 3 medium cloves garlic, crushed
- 3 ounces Parmesan cheese, grated

DIRECTIONS

1. Peel and cut potatoes into small chunks. *(Two potatoes per serving is a good rule-of-thumb. It is best if all pieces are close to the same size.)*
2. Place chunks in a large saucepan, cover with water and add salt.
3. Bring to a boil over medium-high heat and then reduce heat to maintain a slow boil.
4. Cook until potatoes fall apart when pierced with a fork – approximately 30 minutes.
5. When potatoes are almost done, combine half-and-half, butter, and garlic in a medium saucepan – cook over medium heat until the mixture comes to a boil.
6. Remove from heat and set aside.
7. When potatoes are tender, drain water.
8. Using an electric hand mixer, whip the potatoes and slowly add garlic/butter/cream mixture.
9. Stir in the Parmesan cheese and continue to mix until smooth.
10. Cover with foil, let stand for 5 minutes so flavors will blend completely before serving.

RECIPE NOTES

- For plain mashed potatoes – follow the recipe exactly but omit the garlic and cheese.

Green Beans with Almonds

6 Servings – 80 Calories per serving

Tender fresh greens beans are one of the best vegetables - especially when topped with butter, a touch of garlic, and slivered almonds. Be sure not to overcook and serve hot. Delicious!

INGREDIENTS

- 1½ lbs. green beans (as fresh as possible)
- ½ chicken stock
- 1 tablespoon butter (not margarine)
- 2 medium cloves garlic, minced
- ¼ cup slivered almonds
- 1 tablespoon shallots, chopped (Substitute ½ small onion)

DIRECTIONS

1. Trim and cut string beans to your preference – whole, cut in 2" pieces, or julienne *(long vertical strips about the size of a matchstick)*.

2. Place prepared beans in a large skillet and cover with chicken stock – bring to boil.

3. Immediately reduce heat, cover with a lid.

4. Cook until beans are tender, but still crisp, approximately 5 to 7 minutes for julienne strips or 10 to 15 minutes for whole or cut beans.

5. Melt butter in a small skillet - add garlic, almonds, and shallots (onions).

6. Sauté until shallots are glazed and golden - DO NOT brown!

7. When shallots are glazed, turn heat to VERY low - to keep warm.

8. When beans are tender, drain all liquid and pour butter and the glazed shallots over the beans.

9. Toss until beans are well-coated.

10. Place in a warmed bowl or on a warmed plate and serve immediately.

Jiffy® Corn Casserole

Recipe makes 8 Servings – 355 Calories per serving

This is the perfect side dish for any holiday meal, great for anytime you want to impress dinner guests or delicious all by itself. It is a yummy quick-mix, no-fail corn casserole recipe that is extremely versatile. Change it up with the simple variations shown below. I rarely use mixes; this is an exception.

INGREDIENTS

- 8 ounces Jiffy® Corn Muffin mix
- 15 ounces whole kernel corn, drained
- 15 ounces creamed corn, not drained
- 1 cup sour cream
- ½ cup melted butter

DIRECTIONS

1. Preheat the oven to 350° F. and melt the butter.
2. Place all ingredients into a large bowl and mix well.
3. Pour the mixture into a buttered 8 X 8-inch baking pan – and bake uncovered in preheated oven for 45 minutes or until lightly browned.

VARIATIONS

- Add 1 or 2 cage-free eggs to the mixture – this makes a lighter, fluffier corn casserole (and adds a little protein).
- Add ½ to 1 cup shredded cheddar cheese to the mixture – for all the cheese lovers in your world.
- Add ¼ cup sugar to make a sweet corn casserole.
- If you add 2 eggs and ½ cup sugar, it is almost a corn cake. You could serve it for dessert!

Mexican Red Rice

6 Servings – 255 Calories per serving

Mexican Red Rice is a part of a traditional Mexican meal. It makes a delicious accompaniment to steak, chicken, and Mexican entrées such as tacos and enchiladas. (See Mama's Legacy, Volume V, Mexican Favorites)

INGREDIENTS

- 2 tablespoons vegetable oil
- 1 small onion, chopped
- 1 small green pepper, minced
- 1½ cup long-grain rice
- 3 large cloves garlic, finely chopped
- 2½ cups chicken broth
- 1/8 teaspoon Cayenne pepper (adjust to taste)
- 1 cup tomato sauce
- 4 heaping tablespoons fresh parsley, finely chopped
- Salt and pepper, to taste *(be careful, may not need much)*

DIRECTIONS

1. In a medium saucepan, heat oil over medium heat.
2. Add in the fresh onion and green pepper and sauté for 1-2 minutes until softened.
3. Add dry rice and cook with the onions and peppers for about 5 minutes or until rice is golden brown.
4. Add the garlic and sauté for 1 minute more.
5. Add in broth and tomato sauce *(add slowly into the rice, not directly onto the hot pan)*.
6. Add cayenne pepper.

7. Add the parsley if you're using it.
8. Stir and bring to a boil.
9. Once it starts boiling, turn the heat to low and cover. Let it simmer for 20 minutes and fluff with a fork.

RECIPE NOTES

- One (1) cup of unseasoned chopped stewed tomatoes with liquid or canned diced tomatoes with liquid can be substituted for the tomato sauce.
- Salsa is also an acceptable substitute for the tomato sauce.
- You can also add cooked peas and diced carrots to the rice (be sure they are warmed through) just before serving.

Orange Glazed Carrots

6 Servings – 85 Calories per serving

This incredibly delicious recipe is also relatively low-calorie. ENJOY!

INGREDIENTS

- 1½ lb. carrots, trimmed, peeled, and thinly sliced
- 4½ teaspoons orange marmalade (low-calorie is optional)
- 1 teaspoon butter
- Dash ground nutmeg

DIRECTIONS

1. Prepare and steam the carrots.
2. Place marmalade, butter, and nutmeg in a skillet over low heat so that butter begins to melt.
3. When carrots are almost tender (about 7 to 10 minutes), drain and spoon into the warm skillet with the marmalade glaze.

4. Cook, stirring occasionally until carrots are well-coated.
5. Serve immediately.

Patrician Potatoes

6 Servings – 295 Calories per serving

Patrician Potatoes are a must-have during the holidays – but are great as a side dish any time of the year.

INGREDIENTS

- 2½ medium potatoes, peeled and quartered
- 2 tablespoons butter, melted (Not margarine)
- 1 package cream cheese (4 oz), softened
- ½ cup sour cream
- 1 teaspoon salt
- 1 teaspoon fresh chives, minced

- ¼ cup Parmesan cheese
- ½ teaspoon paprika (optional)

DIRECTIONS

1. Preheat oven to 350° F.
2. Generously butter a 9 X 9-inch baking dish.
3. Wash, peel, and cut potatoes into pieces – should be as close to the same size as possible.
4. Place potatoes in a heavy two-quart saucepan and cover with water.
5. Bring to a boil and simmer for 20-30 minutes until tender.
6. When potatoes are almost done, whip the cream cheese, sour cream, and salt in a small bowl until light and fluffy, set aside.
7. When potatoes are tender, drain, place in a large bowl, add butter and whip with an electric beater.
8. Add cream cheese/sour cream mixture to potatoes and whip again.
9. Stir in chives.
10. Spread evenly in prepared baking dish.
11. Sprinkle with parmesan cheese and paprika.
12. Bake, uncovered, at 350° for 20-25 minutes or until heated through.

RECIPE NOTES

- The recipe can be easily doubled to serve 12 – bake in 9 X 13-inch buttered dish.

Rice Pilaf

4 Servings – 160 Calories per serving

Rice pilafs are made by cooking rice briefly in butter or oil before adding water or broth. This technique ensures that the rice grains will be fluffy and separate. This recipe is a basic pilaf. There are many variations. Once you get the hang of it, you can be as creative as you want to be.

INGREDIENTS

- 1 cup long-grain white rice – preferably basmati or jasmine
- 2 tablespoons butter
- ½ cup green onion, chopped *(chopped yellow onion will also work)*
- ½ cup celery, in very thin slices
- 2 cups chicken (or vegetable) stock. The amount will vary depending on the type of rice you are using

- Seasoned salt or plain salt *(use only as needed – ½ teaspoon if using water instead of stock)*
- 1/8 teaspoon freshly ground black pepper
- 1/8 teaspoon Cayenne pepper
- 2 tablespoons fresh parsley, chopped

DIRECTIONS

Cook the Rice

1. Always read the directions on the rice package carefully to determine if the rice you have chosen needs any special preparation, e.g. soaking, rinsing, etc.
2. The directions will also give you the ratio of water to rice that is required for the type of rice you are using.
3. Rice can be cooked in water, chicken or vegetable stock, or a combination of water and stock.
4. My preference is to cook rice in liquid that is primarily stock. As *a rule of thumb*, at least half of the needed liquid should be stock.
5. Homemade stock is always the best choice, if available, and will make a big difference in the quality of the finished product.
6. Place the correct amount of liquid in a 2-quart saucepan (minimum size) – and heat.
7. While the stock is heating, place the butter in a large skillet on medium-high heat. Swirl the pan so the bottom of the pan is completely coated.
8. Add the onions and celery.
9. Cook and stir until golden, about 8 minutes.
10. Add the rice, a little salt - stir until rice is well-coated, about 3 minutes.
11. Check your liquid – if using all water, you will need to add ½ teaspoon salt.

12. If you are using canned or boxed broth, be careful of how much seasoning you add. Is it probably seasoned and will need little, if any, additional salt.
13. Carefully stir-in the slightly browned rice and veggies into the stock.
14. Bring to a simmer, reduce the heat, cover, and cook as directed on the rice package. Usually between 15 to 25 minutes. Use a timer.
15. After cooking for the required amount of time, remove the pan from the heat (do not remove the lid).
16. Let the cooked rice sit for 10 minutes. *At no point during the cooking of the rice should you lift the lid.*
17. Fluff with a fork to serve.
18. Stir in chopped parsley.
19. You can also mix in corn kernels (well-heated), toasted almonds, chopped walnuts, or raisins to the pilaf to make it more interesting.
20. There are many combinations you can use for rice pilaf once you master the basics in this recipe.

Rice with Fresh Corn and Cherry Tomatoes

6 Servings – 302 Calories per serving

Rice with lightly sautéed fresh corn and cherry tomatoes . . . wow, what could be better – colorful and delicious.

INGREDIENTS

- 1 cup raw white rice (Basmati or Jasmine are preferred)
- 1 cube chicken bouillon
- 2 tablespoons butter (not margarine)
- 1 tablespoon olive oil
- 1 medium onion, chopped
- 3 large cloves garlic, minced
- 2 cups cherry tomatoes, washed well and cut in half
- 1 teaspoon sugar, more to taste
- 4 cobs fresh corn (kernels only).
- 1 teaspoon dried or fresh parsley
- 1 teaspoon dried basil
- Salt and pepper, to taste
- Parmesan cheese, grated (to serve on the side)

DIRECTIONS

1. Shuck and parboil fresh corn-on-the-cob for two to three minutes in boiling water.
2. Cool under running cold water and cut kernels from the cobs; set aside.
3. Cook rice according to package directions with chicken bouillon cube added to the water.

4. While rice is cooking, add oil and butter to a large skillet, heat on medium-high heat.

5. Sauté the onions and garlic in butter/oil mixture until soft - about 2 minutes.

6. Add the cherry tomatoes and sauté for 2 or 3 minutes more.

7. Mix sugar, parsley, basil, salt, and pepper in a small bowl.

8. Sprinkle mixed seasonings onto the vegetable mixture in the skillet and stir thoroughly.

9. Immediately add corn kernels to the skillet and sauté for 1 minute more.

10. Add cooked rice to the skillet - cook and stir until rice is heated through.

11. Serve immediately.

12. Provide grated parmesan cheese to sprinkle on top, as desired.

RECIPE NOTES

- Any type of corn will work - try different kinds and find your preference.
- SUBSTITUTIONS - 11 oz can of chipotle white corn (drained) or 10 oz package of frozen loose corn kernels.

Roasted New Potatoes

6 Servings – 183 Calories per serving

These potatoes are wonderful served hot; but, can also be chilled and served with fried chicken or ham as tasty picnic fare.

INGREDIENTS

- 1½ lbs. new red potatoes, scrubbed and dried
- ¼ cup high-quality extra-virgin olive oil
- 4 to 6 large cloves garlic, crushed
- Salt and freshly ground black pepper, use a light touch
- 1 tablespoon fresh parsley, finely chopped

DIRECTIONS

1. Preheat oven to 350° F.
2. If using small potatoes, you will – wash and scrub each potato and score with a knife around the middle of each potato.
3. If using larger new potatoes, you will not need as many – wash, scrub and cut into halves or quarters, depending on size.
4. In a large bowl mix the oil, garlic, and parsley; add the potatoes and toss well.
5. Place potatoes into a shallow baking pan and roast until potatoes are tender when tested with a fork.

RECIPE NOTES

- Other fresh herbs can be substituted for parsley, depending on your personal taste.

Steamed Vegetables

6 Servings – Minimal calories per serving unless adding butter or toppings

You can steam a single vegetable, such as carrots, broccoli, or asparagus, or you can prepare a medley. They can be served hot au natural with salt and pepper or dressed up with olive oil or butter and fresh garlic, melted cheese, or a creamy cheese or butter sauce. Steamed vegetables are always a perfect side dish. They are also a perfect, colorful main dish for lunch when served with fresh hot cornbread and honey-butter.

The chart of the next page lists some of my favorites, but there are many more.

Available Year-Round and Delicious

Carrots

Broccoli & Cauliflower

Brussel Sprouts

Green Peas, shelled

Snow Peas

Zucchini/Yellow Squash

HERBS & SEASONING

Basil, Parsley, Dill, Thyme, Lemon Grass, Hot Pepper
Flakes, Cilantro, Curry Powder or Curry Paste, Garlic
Salt

SPRING & SUMMER FAVORITES	TOPPINGS
Summer Squash	Extra-virgin olive oil and/or Butter with finely chopped onions and a light touch of minced garlic
Green Beans	Cheese: Monterey Jack, Cheddar, Colby, Mozzarella, Gouda, Fresh Mexican Cheese
Thick-Walled Sweet Peppers	Freshly grated Parmesan or Romano to finish off some of the milder cheeses such as Monterey Jack
Whole-Pod Baby Okra	Crumbled bacon with a little of the bacon grease

See chart below: Steaming Times for Vegetables

VEGGIE COOKING cheat sheet

DomesticSuperhero.com

VEGETABLE	BOILED	STEAMED	BAKED/ROASTED	MICROWAVED
Asparagus	Not Recommended	8-10 min	400°F for 8-10 min	2-4 min
Beans	6-8 min	5-8 min	425°F for 12-15 min	3-4 min
Brussels Sprouts	Bring to a boil, simmer 5-7 min	8-10 min	400°F for 20 min	4-6 min
Broccoli	4-6 min	5-6 min	425°F for 15-18 min	2-3 min
Cabbage (shredded)	5-10 min	5-8 min	400°F for 30 min (wedges)	5-6 min
Carrots	5-10 min	4-5 min	400°F for 20-30 min (baby carrots)	4-5 min
Cauliflower	5-10 min	5-10 min	400°F for 25-30 min	2-3 min
Corn on the Cob	5-8 min	4-7 min	350°F for 30 min, husks on	1.5-2 min
Eggplant	Not Recommended	5-6 min	425°F for 25-30 min	2-4 min
Mushrooms	Not Recommended	4-5 min	400°F for 25 min	2-3 min
Onions (sliced)	30-50 min (whole, outer layer removed)	5 min	425°F for 25-30 min (halved)	Not Recommended
Peas	8-12 min	4-5 min	400°F for 20 min	2-3 min
Peppers	Not Recommended	2-4 min	450°F for 15 min or until block (peel skin after)	2-3 min
Potatoes (cut)	15-20 min	10-12 min	425°F for 20 min	6-8 min
Spinach	2-5 min	5-6 min	450°F for 3-6 min	1-2 min
Sweet Potato (cubes)	20-30 min	5-7 min	350°F for 20 min	8 min (whole)
Zucchini	3-5 min	4-6 min	450°F for 12-15 min	2-3 min

Domestic Superhero
Cooking • DIY • Home • Life

190

DIRECTIONS

1. Clean all vegetables thoroughly, peel those that need to be peeled, trim ends, etc., cut to relatively the same-sized pieces.
2. Organize the veggies in order of the length of time required to cook.
3. Start your preparation work with the longest-cooking vegetable, like carrots or winter squash cubes.
4. Then go to the next one – possibly cauliflower.
5. Finally, chop the quick-cooking ones like zucchini or snow peas. Learning the times and what is required to cook each one to perfection is an art. *(See chart above)* It may take a few tries before you get it right – and love the result.
6. When you are nearing the end of chopping, start cooking the vegetable that will take the longest.
7. Have steaming pot ready – filled with water, heat on low, and ready to go with the steamer in place.
8. Turn the heat to medium and put in your first vegetable – layering it across the bottom of the steamer.
9. With bite-sized pieces, allow about two minutes of cook time between the placement of each additional layer to be cooked.

RECIPE NOTES

Crunchy or well-cooked is always the question!

- There are many people (like me) who will only eat vegetables if they can hear and taste a little crunch. As a result, I always err on the side of crunchy. There is nothing less appetizing than mushy, overcooked vegetables.
- Others want their vegetable soft and cooked through – to the point of mushy. You are the cook and know your family, so, you make that decision.

- **RECOMMENDATION**: Try to catch the vegetables when they are just this side of ready (as your family prefers), knowing they will cook a bit more even after being removed from the stove or steamer.
- **GENERAL TIP**: When cooking carrots, tomatoes, or peas, add a scant teaspoon of sugar to enhance their natural flavor - and always go easy on herbs and spices!

SERVING SUGGESTIONS

- Regardless of the season when serving my family steamed vegetables, they are always tossed in olive oil and butter in which I have sautéed several cloves of crushed garlic *(I learned this in Spain)*.
- If there is fresh basil available, it becomes a seasoning star. On a lucky day, there are mushrooms to sauté along with the garlic and basil.
- Use enough oil/butter to give your vegetables a light covering.
- You can also smother them with cheese that melts down through the vegetables and holds them together. Use only good quality, real cheese, do not use spreads or imitation cheese.
- Always serve immediately while piping hot.

COOKING UTENSILS

- This recipe calls for a stove-top steamer.
- I prefer an electric steamer, which is easier to control. Either type works very well. Check Amazon. You can find all sizes and styles (electric or stovetop).

Twice-Baked Potatoes

8 Servings (1/2 shell per serving) – 194 Calories per serving

This is a potato recipe that my family has enjoyed for years. If you have not already discovered it, you are in for a real treat. The potatoes can be prepared ahead and reheated when you are ready to serve. They are exceptionally yummy because butter and cheese are part of the filling.

INGREDIENTS

- 4 large potatoes, unpeeled - Idaho or russet baking potatoes *(8 to 10 oz. each)*
- ¼ to ½ cup milk
- ¼ cup butter
- ¼ teaspoon salt
- Dash freshly ground black pepper
- ½ cup cheddar cheese, grated *(4 oz.)*
- 1 tablespoon fresh chives, finely chopped

DIRECTIONS

1. Pre-heat oven to 375° F.
2. Gently scrub potatoes, but do not peel.
3. Pierce potatoes several times with a fork to allow steam to escape while potatoes bake – and to prevent bursting.
4. Bake 1 hour to 1 hour 15 minutes or until potatoes are tender when pierced in center with a fork.
5. When potatoes are cool enough to handle, cut lengthwise in half; carefully scoop out inside, leaving a thin shell.
6. In a medium bowl, mash potatoes with a potato masher or electric mixer on low speed until completely smooth.
7. Add milk in small amounts, beating after each addition with an electric mixer on low speed *(amount of milk needed to make potatoes smooth and fluffy will vary, depending on the kind of potatoes used)*.
8. Add butter, salt, and pepper; beat vigorously until potatoes are light and fluffy.
9. Stir in cheese and chives.
10. Fill the 8 potato shells with mashed potato mixture.
    (Potatoes can be stored in the refrigerator (covered) at this point until you are ready to serve.)
11. Place on an ungreased cookie sheet.
12. Increase oven temperature to 400°F.
13. Bake about 20 minutes or until hot through.

Zucchini and Onions

4 Servings – 85 Calories per serving

This is a wonderful variation on steamed zucchini, which my granddaughter loves.

INGREDIENTS

- 2 to 3 large zucchinis, scrubbed, scraped (not peeled), ends removed and thinly sliced
- 1 small Vidalia onion, peeled, trimmed, and finely diced or sliced
- ½ teaspoon salt
- Water to cover vegetables
- 1 tablespoon butter
- Freshly ground black pepper
- Garlic salt to taste (optional)

DIRECTIONS

1. Place zucchini and onion in a medium saucepan, cover with water,
2. Cooked until zucchini is tender and falling apart ~15 minutes.
3. Drain completely.
4. Place in a bowl, add butter, and sprinkle very lightly with garlic salt and freshly ground black pepper.

RECIPE NOTES

- *Variation:* Sauté zucchini in butter rather than boiling – or, cook in a steamer.
- Cook the onions in 1 tablespoon Extra-virgin olive oil and 1 tablespoon butter until tender, then add the zucchini.
- Stir until well-blended, cover and cook over low heat until tender.
- Add 1 or 2 tablespoons of water, if necessary.
- Serve with freshly grated parmesan cheese as a topping.

SNACKS

What is a cookbook for singles without snacks? Some of the recipes I included are healthier than others; but I wanted to give you a variety.

They are mostly on the sweet side, but there are a few that are loaded with nutrients and also taste great like the Energy Bites.

For something different and delicious, indulge yourself with the Spanish Hot Chocolate.

Homemade sweet snacks tend to be healthier than the packaged variety because you can control the ingredients. Homemade will not be filled with additives and a lot of "added sugars." You can also use whole-wheat flour without changing the flavor. No one will be able to tell the difference.

Enjoy making them and enjoy eating them – I know, I do!

Banana Chocolate Chip Bites

20 Energy Bites – 87 Calories per bite

Finding healthy snack foods can be challenging. The temptation to eat the "horrible" foods from the vending machines can be great. It is important to keep good foods available to grab and eat when you are hungry and need to give your body extra exergy. This is one of those good snacks! Make a batch and freeze – then they will be readily available when you need them.

INGREDIENTS

- 1¼ cup rolled oats
- 1 tablespoon chia seeds or wheat germ
- ⅓ cup maple syrup
- ¼ cup almond butter
- 1 ripe banana, mashed
- 1 teaspoon pure vanilla extract
- 1 teaspoon ground cinnamon
- ¼ cup semi-sweet chocolate chips

DIRECTIONS

1. Mix all ingredients in a medium to a large bowl.
2. Cover the bowl and let the batter sit in the fridge at least three hours or overnight. The batter will be sticky; but it will firm up as it sits.
3. With damp hands press the mixture into 20 energy balls.
4. Cover lightly with wax paper and place the prepared energy balls in the fridge for at least two hours – preferably overnight. They will become firm as they chill.
5. Great for breakfast, a quick snack, or as a healthy treat in lunch boxes.

6.   Refrigerate for up to 5-6 days – or freeze up to three months. Best if the bites thaw at room temperature for 20 minutes before eating.

Best Banana Bread

10 Servings – 282 calories per serving

What is that wonderful aroma in the kitchen? Must be Mom's banana bread. Such a perfect treat to take to work for a late afternoon snack. It's also a great dessert with a little vanilla ice cream, maybe for breakfast with a glass of cold milk, or a favorite bedtime snack. So many choices! The best part of all – you can whip it up in no time.

INGREDIENTS

- 1 cube butter
- 1 cup sugar
- 2 eggs, lightly beaten
- 4 bananas, mashed well
- 1½ cups whole wheat flour
- 1 teaspoon baking soda
- ½ teaspoon salt
- ½ teaspoon vanilla

DIRECTIONS

1. Preheat oven to 350º F.
2. Cream butter and sugar.
3. Add eggs and crushed bananas and mix well.
4. Place flour, soda, and salt in a medium bowl and whisk to blend.
5. Add to creamed mixture.
6. Stir in vanilla and mix just until combined. Do not overmix.
7. Pour into a greased and floured loaf pan.
8. Bake in preheated oven for 55 minutes.
9. Cool on a wire rack and remove from pan.

10. It can be eaten warm or cold.

11. Refrigerate or freeze leftover bread.

Gingerbread Muffins

6 muffins – 218 Calories per muffin

This classic Southern recipe is perfect for a cold winter's night when a sweet treat is in order. In only makes six muffins. You can mix them up in a flash, 15-20 minutes to bake, sprinkle with a little powdered sugar, and enjoy. Your roomies or that special someone will love you for being so handy in the kitchen!

If you need 12 muffins, instead of six, the recipe doubles easily.

INGREDIENTS

- 1/3 cup light brown sugar
- 1/3 cup molasses (DO NOT use Blackstrap)
- 1/3 cup boiling water
- 2 tablespoons unsalted butter, softened
- ½ teaspoon baking soda
- ¼ teaspoon salt

- 1 large egg yolk (egg white reserved for another use)
- ¾ cup all-purpose flour
- 1 teaspoon ground ginger
- ½ teaspoon ground cinnamon
- 1/8 teaspoon ground nutmeg
- 1/8 teaspoon ground allspice
- 1/8 teaspoon ground cloves
- Powdered sugar for sprinkling

DIRECTIONS

1. Preheat the oven to 350° F.
2. Place 6 cupcake liners in the wells of a 6-well muffin pan.
3. Using a wire whisk, mix the brown sugar, molasses, boiling water, and butter in a medium-sized glass bowl.
4. Continue to stir until the butter melts and mixes in completely.
5. Add baking soda and salt.
6. Set the mixture aside to cool for 10 minutes, stirring occasionally.
7. Beat in the egg yolk.
8. Measure and mix the flour and spices in a separate bowl.
9. Add this to the molasses mixture and whisk to combine.
10. Divide the mixture between the muffin cups.
11. Bake on a rack in the lower third of the oven for 15 minutes.
12. Test for doneness with a toothpick. Moist crumbs should cling to the toothpick; but if the toothpick is wet, you may need to bake for another 3-5 minutes.
13. They can be eaten immediately (if you can't wait) – so tasty with real butter).
14. They are also wonderful if you allow them to cool and store in an air-tight container overnight to be enjoyed the next day.

Guacamole

4 Servings – 177 Calories per serving

I grew up in Arizona and love Mexican food. Guacamole is not only easy to prepare and delicious, it is also good for you. It is perfect for a snack or as the first part of a Mexican dinner – or anytime with a bag of tortilla chips and cold beer.

INGREDIENTS

- 2 large (about 8 oz) ripe avocados, peeled and seed removed
- 1½ limes, juice only
- 1 medium tomato, washed, ends removed, and finely diced
- ½ medium white onion, chopped fine

- 1/8 teaspoon freshly ground pepper
- ¼ teaspoon salt
- 1 large clove garlic, minced
- Large dash cumin
- Large dash cayenne pepper
- Pinch of sugar
- 1/3 bunch fresh cilantro, finely chopped without stems
- ½ serrano chili (optional), finely chopped

DIRECTIONS

1. Place peeled and pitted avocados in a large flat bowl.
2. Mash with a fork – OK to leave a few small chunks.
3. Mix in all remaining ingredients.
4. Serve immediately with plenty of fresh tortilla chips.

   (Avocado will go dark if left standing.)

Homemade Caramel Corn

Caramel corn is a childhood favorite for many people. This sweet and crunchy, tasty treat will be enjoyed by you and all your friends. Great for parties, or just enjoy for a stay-at-home night in front of the TV.

INGREDIENTS

- 6 quarts popped popcorn
- 2 cups packed light brown sugar
- 1 cup butter, cut in chunks
- ½ cup light corn syrup
- 1 teaspoon salt
- 3 teaspoons vanilla extract
- ½ teaspoon baking soda

DIRECTIONS

Prepare the Popcorn

1. Preheat oven to 250° F.
2. Generously butter two 13 X 9-inch baking pans; set aside.
3. Pop the corn (do not salt).
4. Remove un-popped kernels (be sure you get all of them); set aside.

Make the caramel

1. Combine the sugar, butter, corn syrup, and salt in a large heavy-duty saucepan.
2. Bring to a boil over medium heat, stirring constantly (don't leave the mixture on the stove. It could burn or bubble over).
3. Continue boiling for 5 minutes, stirring occasionally.
4. Remove from the heat; stir in vanilla and baking soda *(There will be steam and a color change when the soda is added, so be careful.)*
5. Stir to mix well.

Make the Caramel Corn

1. Pour over popped popcorn and stir until well-coated.
2. Spread coated popcorn evenly in two greased 13×9-in. baking pans.
3. Bake, uncovered for 45 minutes, stirring every 15 minutes.
4. Cool completely.
5. Store in zip-top plastic bags or an airtight container to maintain freshness.

RECIPE NOTES

- Have fun with the recipe.
- Try adding your favorite nuts, chocolate pieces, and dried fruit to the popcorn before coating.

Protein Energy Bites

24 Energy Bites – 71 Calories per bite

Easy, no-bake, healthy, energy-filled snacks, made with all-natural ingredients. Perfect for school lunches. Place frozen bites in a plastic bag. They will thaw and be ready to eat by lunchtime.

INGREDIENTS (BASIC RECIPE)

- Softened butter
- ½ cup pure peanut butter
- 1 cup old-fashioned oats
- 1 cup chopped raw almonds/pecans/walnuts *(your choice)*
- ¼ cup organic honey
- ¼ cup chocolate chips (optional)

DIRECTIONS

1. Lightly butter each mini muffin well.
2. Place all ingredients in a large bowl and stir with a sturdy wooden spoon.
3. Mix until well blended.
4. Refrigerate for at least one hour.
5. Use a cookie scoop or tablespoon to place the mixture into each mini muffin well.
6. Freeze for at least three hours.
7. Remove from pan.
8. Thaw and serve.

NOTE: If the energy bites stick to the pan, set the pan in warm water for one minute.

RECIPE NOTES

- The bites can be stored in the refrigerator for up to one week or frozen for up to 2 months.
- If you don't have a min-muffin pan, you can roll into balls.

Change-up the Recipe for Fun

- Replace peanut butter with almond butter.
- Use ¾ cup dried blueberries, cranberries, or cherries mixed with ½ cup sliced almonds and a dash of cinnamon instead of nuts only.
- Use 1/3 cup dried cherries, 1/3 cup chocolate chips, and 1/3 cup chopped pecans with 1 tablespoon cocoa powder.
- Use ¼ cup almond butter instead of peanut butter with 1 cup chopped walnuts, 1/3 cup chopped pitted dates, and ¼ to 1/3 cup maple syrup instead of honey.

Spanish Style Hot Chocolate

4 Servings - 261 Calories per serving

Thick, smooth Spanish hot chocolate (from Spain) is an elegant take on one of America's favorite drinks. My first experience with this amazing drink was 50 years ago when I was a young married living in Madrid, Spain. With my first sip, I thought I had died and gone to Heaven. If you want to impress a special friend – this is the way to do it!

INGREDIENTS

- 3 cups whole milk
- 1 cup evaporated milk
- ½ teaspoon pure vanilla extract
- ¼ cup unsweetened cocoa powder
- ¼ cup sugar
- ¼ cup cornstarch
- ¼ teaspoon cinnamon

DIRECTIONS

1. Combine the whole milk, evaporated milk, and vanilla in a heavy saucepan.

2. Place over low heat and stir occasionally until it is warm – don't let it boil.

3. Combine the cocoa powder, sugar, cornstarch, and cinnamon in a bowl and whisk to combine.

4. Whisk the cocoa mixture into the warm milk mixture and continue whisking until smooth.

5. Bring to a boil, whisking frequently to prevent it from scorching.

6. Remove the hot chocolate from the heat just after it has come to a boil.

7. The mixture should be super-rich and thick!

8. Serve immediately – no need for marshmallows or whipped cream; especially good with Churros *(Try Trader Joe's)*.

DESSERTS

Is there anything better than a melt-in-your-mouth dessert. I don't think so. ***You have just hit the jackpot of dessert recipes.***

Some of them have been in my family for 50 years, or more; and others, I recently discovered. The new ones have all been tested, many with the help of my granddaughter, Bella. Her favorite recipe is the Chocolate Mayonnaise Cupcakes. (I promise you can't taste the mayonnaise.)

Cookies are always a big hit, whether you make them to satisfy your sweet tooth, or for a party. You have the Original Toll House Cookie recipe and several variations. Each is unique and delicious on its own.

Other family favorites are Chocolate Ice Cream pie and The World's Best Cheesecake. Both are incredibly easy to make and will receive high praise from family and friends.

If you enjoy making "old" things new again, try The Hummingbird Skillet Cake. This is a new version of an old traditional Southern recipe that I recently discovered through a book I was reading. It is amazing! As the saying goes, "Try it, you'll like it." 😊

Try every recipe and find your favorites. I would love to hear which ones win your praises. Email me at nancy@nancynwilson.com. Looking forward to hearing about your cooking adventures.

All Shook-Up Ice Cream

1 Serving – 278 Calories per serving (with ½ cup fresh strawberries)

This recipe can be a fun activity at a party or family gathering. It is especially good for younger children – although, a big group of grown-up friends may also enjoy the fun!

INGREDIENTS (PER SERVING)
- 1 tablespoon sugar
- ½ cup heavy cream
- ¼ teaspoon vanilla
- 6 tablespoons rock salt
- 1 pint-sized Ziploc® plastic bag
- 1 gallon-sized Ziploc® plastic bag
- Plenty of ice
- Bag of rock salt

DIRECTIONS
1. Fill the gallon plastic bag half-full of ice and add 6 tablespoons rock salt.
2. Place sugar, cream, and vanilla in the small Ziploc bag and seal it completely (double-check seal).
3. Place the small bag filled with ingredients inside the large bag and seal it completely (double-check seal).
4. Give the bag to one person and instruct him/her to shake until the mixture has turned into ice cream, about 6-8 minutes.
5. Remove the small bag from the larger one and rinse.
6. Hand them a spoon, open the bag carefully, and let them enjoy the result of their effort.

7. OPTIONAL: Have fresh fruit (crushed strawberries or pineapple) and nuts to add to the finished product.

RECIPE NOTES

- It is a good idea to have the small bags all prepared and in the refrigerator.
- Also, have the ice bags prepared and in the freezer.
- Be prepared it will make the set up easy – just put them together and pass them out. Enjoy the fun!

Avocado Brownies

16 Servings – 138 Calories per serving

Brownies are so American, who doesn't love them? This recipe is even better than the norm because it has a secret, healthy ingredient, avocado. Try them, you will love them.

INGREDIENTS

- 4 eggs
- ¾ cup sugar
- ¾ cup brown sugar
- ½ cup flour
- 1¼ cocoa powder, sifted
- 2 teaspoons vanilla extract
- ½ teaspoon salt
- 2 ripe avocados, mashed (about 1 cup)

DIRECTIONS

1. Preheat oven to 350° F.

2. Grease and flour an 8-inch square baking pan.

3. In a large bowl, beat eggs at medium speed until light yellow and fluffy.

4. Add both sugars and combine just until blended.

5. Add remaining ingredients and beat on low speed to combine.

6. Pour brownie batter into baking pan.

7. Bake for 30-35 minutes or until a toothpick comes out clean.

8. Allow to cool before serving.

Best Apple Pie

10 Servings – 287 Calories per serving

Apple pie and pumpkin pie are two traditional recipes that must be included in any good cookbook. You will find both recipes in this book. I promise they are tried and true, beloved family favorites that you and your friends will enjoy.

INGREDIENTS

- 1 unbaked pastry for 9" two-crust pie
- 6 cups apples, pared, cored, and sliced very thin *(Granny Smith Apples are the best!)*
- ½ to 2/3 cup sugar *(Very tart apples require the larger amount)*
- ¼ teaspoon salt
- 1½ tablespoon cornstarch
- ¼ teaspoon cinnamon
- 1/8 teaspoon ground nutmeg
- 2 tablespoon real butter
- 1 tablespoon lemon juice – freshly squeezed
- 1 teaspoon vanilla extract

DIRECTIONS

1. Prepare pie crust for double-crust pie *(homemade or refrigerated prepared pie crusts)*.
2. Line a 9" pie plate with one crust.
3. Pre-heat oven to 450° F.
4. Pare, core, and slice the apples.
5. In a large bowl, combine and sift all dry ingredients.
6. Add sliced apples and stir gently until apples are well-coated.

7. Place them in layers in the pie shell *(sprinkle remaining dry ingredients in the bowl over the top of the apples)*.

8. Place dots of softened sweet cream butter evenly across the top of the apples.

9. Sprinkle with lemon juice and vanilla - OR - for a tangy secret ingredient taste, sprinkle with 2 teaspoons white wine vinegar.

10. Cover with the top crust, seal, and flute the edges.

11. Prick top with a fork - create your own design.

12. For a sweet touch, lightly sprinkle the top crust with sugar and cinnamon mixture just before baking.

13. Cover the fluted edges with strips of foil to prevent burning *(or use a metal pie edge protector)*.

14. Remove the foil (or protector) for the last 10 minutes of baking.

15. Bake at 450° F. ~ 10 minutes then, reduce heat to 350° F.

16. Bake until done ~ 35-45 additional minutes or until golden brown and bubbly.

RECIPE NOTES

Variations

Apple-Pecan Pie

- Stir in ½ cup chopped pecans with the sugar.
- Increase baking time to 50 to 60 minutes and top with. . .
  CRUNCHY PECAN GLAZE.
  - Place ¼ cup brown sugar (packed); 1/3 cup chopped pecans and 1 tablespoon light cream in a small saucepan. Cook over low heat, stirring constantly, until thick.

Dutch Apple Pie

- Make extra-large slits in the top crust before baking.
- 5 minutes before the pie is done, pour ½ cup heavy cream through the slits and continue baking for the final 5 minutes.
- This pie is best when served warm.

French Apple Pie

- Do not cover with the 2nd crust - use a CRUMB TOPPING (see below).
- Combine 1 cup flour, ½ cup firm butter, and ½ cup brown sugar (packed) - mix with an electric mixer on low speed until the mixture is crumbly.
- Spread evenly across the top of the pie.
- Bake for 50 minutes - covering the topping with foil during the last 10 minutes to prevent burning. This pie is best served warm.

Chocolate Chip Cookies
Original Toll House® Recipe

5 dozen cookies – 108 Calories per cookie

This is the original Toll House® Cookie Recipe from the package. There are dozens of variations you may want to try, but this recipe always works! So, start here and enjoy every scrumptious bite.

INGREDIENTS

- 2¼ cups all-purpose flour
- 1 teaspoon baking soda
- 1 teaspoon salt
- 1 cup (2 sticks) butter, softened

- ¾ cup granulated sugar
- ¾ cup packed brown sugar
- 1 teaspoon vanilla extract
- 2 large eggs
- 2 cups Nestlé® Toll House® Semi-Sweet Chocolate Morsels *(Experiment with Dark Chocolate, White Chocolate, Butterscotch or even a mixture of different flavored morsels)*
- 1 cup chopped nuts (optional)

DIRECTIONS

1. Preheat oven to 375° F.
2. Generously butter two large cookie sheets.
3. Measure and place flour, baking soda, and salt in a small bowl – whisk until blended – set aside.
4. Place the softened butter, granulated sugar, brown sugar, and vanilla extract in a large mixing bowl and beat with a handheld electric mixer until creamy.
5. Add eggs, one at a time, beating well after each addition.
6. Gradually beat in the flour mixture – ½ cup at a time. Beat until well-blended, but don't over mix.
7. Using a wooden spoon, stir in the chocolate morsels and nuts.
8. Use a cookie scoop or a large tablespoon and drop on cookie sheets about 2-3 inches apart.
9. Bake for 9 to 11 minutes or until golden brown.
10. Cool on baking sheets for 2 minutes.
11. Using a pancake turner, remove cookies from pan and let cool on wire racks that have been covered with clean, dry paper towels.
12. Spoon up another batch on the cookie sheets and continue baking until all dough has been used.

COOKING TIPS

- As soon as you remove the cookies from the oven, use two tablespoons to slightly scrunch up the edges. This creates a crispier edge and a softer, chewy center.

- *When using Butterscotch Chips* – use only a scant ¾ cup granulated sugar and increase the brown sugar to 1 cup. It gives the dough a slight caramel taste that compliments the butterscotch chips.

- Dough may be stored in the refrigerator for up to one week or in the freezer for up to eight weeks. Cook whenever the mood strikes you – one cookie sheet batch at a time.

COOKIE BARS (VARIATION)

1. Preheat oven to 350° F.
2. Butter a 15 X 10-inch jelly-roll pan.
3. Prepare cookie dough exactly as described as above through Step 7.
4. Then, spread the dough into a well-buttered pan and bake for 20 to 25 minutes until golden brown.
5. Set the pan on a wire rack to cool.
6. Cut into squares - makes 4 dozen bars.

This recipe is from www.VeryBestBaking.com. Nestle® Toll House® is a registered trademark of Société des Produits Nestlé S.A., Vevey, Switzerland.

Chocolate Chip Cookie Cake

6 Servings – 1135 Calories per serving with frosting, 935 without

A soft, chewy cookie cake filled with chocolate chips and topped with a chocolate buttercream frosting. This is the perfect dessert for a family party or a sleepover with friends.

INGREDIENTS for the Cookie Cake

- 2 cups all-purpose flour
- ½ teaspoon baking soda
- ¾ teaspoon salt
- 1¾ cup unsalted butter, softened
- ¾ cup light brown sugar, packed
- ¼ cup granulated sugar
- 1 large egg, room temperature
- 1 large egg yolk, room temperature
- 1 teaspoon pure vanilla extract
- 1 cup semi-sweet chocolate chips

INGREDIENTS for the Chocolate Butter Cream Frosting

- ½ cup unsalted butter, softened
- 1½ cups powdered sugar
- ¼ cup unsweetened cocoa powder
- 1 to 2 tablespoons half and half
- ½ teaspoon pure vanilla extract
- A small dash of salt

DIRECTIONS

Make the Cookie-Cake

1. Spray a 9-inch springform pan with nonstick cooking spray or grease with softened butter; set aside.
2. In a large mixing bowl, whisk the flour, baking soda, and salt; set aside.
3. Place the butter, brown sugar, and granulated sugar in a large mixing bowl.
4. Using a hand-held electric mixer, beat for 1-2 minutes until the mixture is well-combined and creamy.
5. Add the egg, egg yolk, and vanilla extract.
6. Continue to beat until ingredients are fully blended.
7. Slowly mix in the dry ingredients and continue mixing until just combined, making sure to stop and scrape down the sides of the bowl with a rubber spatula, as needed. (Don't overmix.)
8. With a wooden spoon, gently mix in the chocolate chips.
9. Scoop the cookie dough into the prepared springform pan and spread it out into one even layer.
10. Bake at 350° F for 25-30 minutes or until the top of the cookie cake is set and lightly browned.
    Note: Cover loosely with foil if needed to prevent excess browning on top of the cookie cake.
11. Remove from the oven, set on a wire rack.
12. Allow to cool completely before removing from the pan.

Make the Frosting

1. In a large mixing bowl using a hand-held electric mixer, beat the softened butter on medium speed for 1-2 minutes or until smooth and fluffy.
2. Add the powdered sugar, scrape down the sides of the bowl, then add the cocoa powder and mix until fully combined.

3. Add the heavy whipping cream, vanilla extract, and salt.
4. Beat on medium speed until fully combined, making sure to scrape down the sides of the bowl with a rubber spatula, as needed.
5. Spread the frosting on the cooled cookie cake,
   (The cake can also be served without the frosting and topped with rich vanilla ice cream.)

RECIPE TIPS

- Store leftover cookie cake in an airtight container at room temperature or in the refrigerator for up to four days.
- Cookie cake freezes well for up to 3 months. When ready to serve, thaw overnight in the refrigerator; then, bring to room temperature.
- Make the frosting fresh, no more than a few hours before serving.
- The frosting also freezes well for up to 3 months. Thaw overnight in the refrigerator, bring to room temperature and mix well before frosting the cookie cake.

Chocolate Ice Cream Pie

8 Servings – 1289 Calories per serving without nuts

*Ice Cream Pie has been the **gold star family favorite** in our home since a friend introduced it to us over 40 years ago. It is a "must-have" for the holidays. This should be one of the first on your list to try!*

INGREDIENTS

Chocolate Sauce

- 1 cup semi-sweet chocolate chips
- 1 cup evaporated milk
- 1 cup mini marshmallows
- 1 dash salt
- 1 teaspoon vanilla extract

Other Ingredients

- 1-gallon rich vanilla ice cream
- ½ box vanilla wafers
- ½ cup walnuts, chopped (optional)

DIRECTIONS

Make the Chocolate Sauce

1. Melt chocolate chips, milk, marshmallows, salt, and vanilla over medium heat.
2. Cook until thickened – stirring occasionally to prevent burning.
3. Set aside to cool – must be cool before assembling the pie.

Assemble the Pie

1. Line bottom of the pie plate *(9" preferable)* with vanilla wafers.
2. Place a layer of ice cream over vanilla wafers to form the first layer of ice cream. *(Ice cream must be just soft enough to work with, but not so soft that it will quickly melt into a mushy mess.)*
3. Flatten the ice cream to fill in the gaps and make a solid layer.
4. Spread ½ chocolate sauce over the ice cream - covering completely.
5. Place vanilla wafers around the edge of the pie plate to complete the crust (flat side against the pie plate slanted edge).
6. Build another layer of ice cream *(this should use all or most of the ice cream).*
7. Cover top with remaining chocolate or to taste.
8. Sprinkle top with nuts, if desired.
9. Cover with plastic wrap and place in the freezer to set *(at least four hours before serving.)*
10. Take out of the freezer about 20 minutes before serving to facilitate cutting.

RECIPE NOTES

- For family dinners I make half of the pie topped with nuts and half without - to meet everyone's preferences.
- This is a great holiday or special occasion dessert because it can be made several days ahead of time.
- Just remember to take it out of the freezer 20 minutes before serving so that it will cut easily.

Easy Chocolate Chip Cookies

40 cookies – 153 Calories per cookie

You will love this recipe because it is exactly as the name says EASY. The cookies can be made in minutes and rate at the top of the scale for homemade chocolate chip cookies! Be sure to use the "GRAND" size chocolate chips.

INGREDIENTS

- 1 cup melted butter
- 1 cup packed light brown sugar
- ¾ cup granulated sugar
- 2 large eggs
- 2 teaspoons vanilla extract
- 2½ cups flour
- 1 teaspoon baking soda
- ¾ teaspoon salt
- 2 cups (a 12 oz. bag) *Ghirardelli® Grand Semi-sweet Chocolate Chips*

DIRECTIONS

1. Preheat oven to 375° F.
2. In a large bowl, add the melted butter, brown sugar, and granulated sugar.
3. Whisk until well combined.
4. Add the eggs and vanilla – whisk until smooth.
5. Add the flour, baking soda, and salt.
6. Stir until well-mixed – be careful not to overmix.
7. Stir in the chocolate chips and continue stirring until chips are completely mixed into the dough.

8. Scoop out 1½ tablespoon-size balls of the batter on a baking sheet, leaving 2 inches between each cookie. *(A cookie scoop works well for this.)*

9. Bake for 10 to 12 minutes. The center should be soft, and the edges should barely be golden. DO NOT OVERBAKE.

10. Cool 3-4 minutes on the cookie sheet.

11. With a pancake turner, carefully move the cookies to a wire rack covered with a clean paper towel.

12. When completely cool, store in a sealable plastic bag.

13. If not eating in the next two or three days, freeze for up to 3 months.

14. Thaw at room temperature, or if in a hurry, microwave for 30 seconds (one at a time).

No-bake Chocolate Peanut Butter Oatmeal Cookies

24 Cookies – 174 Calories per cookie

These are simple and fun to make. If you want a quick, no-fuss, no-bother snack to satisfy that sweet craving, this is your go-to recipe.

INGREDIENTS

- ½ cup butter, softened
- 2 cups granulated sugar
- ½ cup milk
- 4 tablespoons unsweetened cocoa
- ½ cup creamy natural peanut butter (well-stirred – be sure no excess oil remains)
- 2 teaspoons vanilla extract (OR - ½ teaspoon almond extract with 1½ teaspoons vanilla)
- 3 cups quick oats (not old-fashioned)

DIRECTIONS

1. Mix the butter, sugar, milk, and cocoa in a large saucepan.
2. Bring to a rolling boil, stirring continuously for 1 minute; remove from heat.
3. Add peanut butter to the hot mixture and stir until melted.
4. Add vanilla extract (or almond/vanilla extract blend).
5. Stir in the oats until well blended.
6. Drop 1 tablespoon at a time onto wax paper.
7. Let cookies cool until set.

Peanut Butter
Chocolate Chip Cookies

24 Cookies – 189 Calories per cookie

This cookie recipe is the best of both worlds! Enjoy the soft-crumbly richness of this cookie. In my family's opinion, this is the most delicious melt-in-your-mouth cookie EVER!

INGREDIENTS

- ½ cup unsalted butter — melted
- ½ cup creamy peanut butter
- ¼ cup granulated sugar
- 2/3 cup packed brown sugar
- ½ teaspoon vanilla extract
- 1 large egg
- ½ teaspoon baking soda
- ½ teaspoon salt
- 1¾ cups all-purpose flour
- 1½ cups chocolate chips

DIRECTIONS

1. Using a hand-held electric mixer on low, blend butter with peanut butter until smooth.
2. Add brown sugar and granulated sugar and continue to mix until creamy.
3. Beat in vanilla, egg, baking soda, and salt.
4. Mix in flour slowly just until cookie dough forms (don't over-mix).
5. Stir in chocolate chips.

6. Scoop 2 tablespoonsful cookie dough balls onto well-greased cookie sheets – pan could be covered with parchment paper or silicone baking mats, rather than greasing them.
7. Chill for 30 minutes.
8. When ready to bake, preheat oven to 350° F.
9. Cross press each cookie with tines of a fork *(traditional peanut butter cookie crosshatch)*.
10. Bake cookies for 8-10 minutes, or until slightly brown on the bottom and the top just loses the wet cookie dough look. Don't overbake.
11. Store in an airtight container for up to 3 days or freeze for up to one month.

RECIPE NOTES

- The dough is different than typical chocolate chip cookies. It tends to fall apart. You will have to roll it into balls before placing them on the cookie sheet.
- Be sure to press each cookie down with the fork tines *(peanut butter cookie style)* because the cookie does not spread as it bakes.

Chocolate Mayonnaise Cupcakes

12 Cupcakes – 117 Calories per cupcake

This is an old family recipe that has been passed down from my grandmother; but the recipe originated in New York City. You DO NOT taste the mayonnaise – and it is an amazing chocolate cake.

INGREDIENTS

- 2 cups all-purpose (or wheat) flour
- 2/3 cup unsweetened cocoa powder
- 1¼ teaspoons baking soda
- ¼ teaspoon baking powder
- 3 cage-free eggs
- 12/3 cups sugar
- 1 teaspoon vanilla extract
- 1 cup Hellmann's® or Best Foods® Real Mayonnaise
- 11/3 cups water

DIRECTIONS

1. Preheat oven to 350° F.
2. Place one cupcake liner in each well of the cupcake pan; set aside.
3. In a medium bowl, combine flour, cocoa, baking soda, and baking powder; set aside.
4. Place eggs, sugar, and vanilla in a large mixing bowl.
5. Beat with a hand-held electric mixer set at high speed for 3 minutes or until light and fluffy.
6. Using low speed, beat in Hellmann's® or Best Foods® Real Mayonnaise – mix until well-blended.
7. Alternately beat in flour mixture and water. Begin and end with flour mixture. Be sure to scrape down the sides with a rubber spatula as you mix.
8. Fill each cupcake liner about ¾ full, which will create a nice rounded top on the cupcake.**
9. Bake 30 minutes or until a toothpick inserted in the center of a cupcake comes out clean.
10. Set on a wire rack to cool for 10 minutes.
11. Remove cupcakes from pans and cool completely.
12. Sprinkle with confectioners' sugar or frost with your favorite frosting

NOTE: My favorite frosting is the next recipe.

** *To BAKE AS A CAKE*

- Prepare batter as directed above and pour into a buttered and lightly floured 9 X 13-inch baking pan.
- Bake 40 minutes or until a toothpick inserted in the center comes out clean.
- Remove cake from the oven and set on a wire rack to let it cool completely before frosting.

Vanilla Butter Cream Frosting

2 Cups frosting – can be doubled easily

This frosting is perfect for almost any dessert that needs frosting such as cake, cupcakes, and cookies. It can also be used to "decorate" Christmas Cookies – just add coloring and sprinkles.

INGREDIENTS

- ½ cup butter (1 stick), softened
- 2 cups powdered sugar, sifted
- 1 teaspoons vanilla
- Dash of salt
- 1-2 tablespoons milk, heavy cream, or half-and-half

DIRECTIONS

1. Place softened butter into a medium-sized bowl.
2. Beat with electric hand-held mixture set on medium until butter is smooth ~3 minutes.
3. Add powdered sugar ½ cup at a time; plus, vanilla and dash of salt.
4. After all the sugar has been mixed in, turn the mixer to high speed and beat about 10 seconds to fluff and lighten the frosting.
5. Add milk, heavy cream or half-and-half until the frosting is a spreadable consistency.
6. If you want a stiffer frosting, add more confectioner's sugar, ¼ cup at a time.
7. If you want softer frosting, add more milk or cream, a tablespoon at a time.

RECIPE NOTES

- To make chocolate frosting, add 1/3 cup unsweetened cocoa as you are mixing in the powdered sugar. *(Powdered sugar is also known as Confectioners' Sugar)*

Devil's Food Cake

10 Servings - 415 Calories per serving (add calories for frosting)

This is one of the best chocolate cakes in the world and a favorite during my young years, then later with my children. It is a light cake, yet deliciously rich and moist.

INGREDIENTS

- 4 ounces unsweetened chocolate
- 1 cup milk
- 1 cup light brown sugar, packed
- 3 large eggs, separated
- 2 cups cake flour, sifted
- 1 teaspoon baking soda
- ½ teaspoon salt
- ¼ cup water
- 1 teaspoon vanilla extract
- ½ cup unsalted butter (1 cube)
- 1 cup sugar

DIRECTIONS

1. Have all ingredients at room temperature.
2. Pre-heat oven to 350° F.
3. Grease and flour two 9" round cake pans.
4. Mix the unsweetened chocolate, ½ cup milk, brown sugar, and one egg yolk in the top of a double boiler
5. Place the pan over the pan of boiling water and cook, stirring constantly until smooth and thickened.
6. Remove from heat and let it cool to room temperature.

7. Place the flour, baking soda and salt in a bowl; mix thoroughly with a wire whisk; set aside.

8. In a small bowl, mix the remaining ½ cup milk, water, and vanilla; set aside.

9. Place the butter in a large bowl and beat with an electric mixer on medium-high speed until creamy, ~30 seconds.

10. Gradually add the sugar and beat until the mixture is light and fluffy ~ 5 minutes.

11. Add two large egg yolks one at a time into the mixture and mix well.

12. Reduce the speed to low and add the flour the mixture in three parts alternating with the milk mixture in two parts - beat until smooth.

13. Stir in the chocolate mixture.

14. Place 2 egg whites in a medium bowl and beat with the electric mixer on medium-high speed until stiff, but not dry.

15. Gently fold the egg whites into the batter.

16. Pour the batter into the two prepared cake pans; smooth the top with a rubber spatula.

17. Bake for about 25 minutes or until a toothpick inserted into the center comes out clean.

18. Cool, remove from the pans and frost with **Vanilla Butter Cream Frosting** shown above or Chocolate Fudge Frosting or Seven-minute White Fluffy Frostings – which can be found in **Cake Making Made Easy**.

Hummingbird Skillet Cake

10 Servings – 361 Calories per serving (without frosting)

Try this classic Southern dessert soon. It looks a little like carrot cake, right down to the light and tangy cream cheese frosting, but the pineapple and banana give it a tropical twist. Be sure to use a cast-iron frying pan as instructed, or it may not turn out well.

INGREDIENTS

- ¾ cup chopped pecan pieces
- 1 small pineapple
- 1 small banana
- ¾ cup sugar (plus 1 tablespoon)
- 1 teaspoon baking powder
- ¾ teaspoons kosher salt (for table salt, use about half as much)
- ½ teaspoon ground cinnamon
- ¼ teaspoon ground cloves

241

- ¼ teaspoon baking soda
- ¼ teaspoon grated nutmeg
- 2 large cage-free eggs, straight from the fridge
- 1½ teaspoon vanilla extract
- ¾ cup unsalted butter, melted
- 1¼ scant cup flour
- 2 cups cream cheese frosting or cream cheese buttercream frosting
- Toasted pecans, to taste

DIRECTIONS

1. Adjust oven rack to the middle position.
2. Preheat oven to 350° F.
3. Have a 10-inch cast-iron skillet ready to be preheated.
4. Toast the pecans on a sheet pan until golden brown, about 5-10 minutes, and cool completely; watch them carefully so they don't scorch. This can be done in advance and stored in an airtight container at room temperature for several weeks.
5. Peel, trim, and core the pineapple.
6. Place 2/3 cup pineapple into a blender, or a tall, narrow jar for an immersion blender.
7. Peel a banana, measure out 1/3 cup and place in the blender.
8. Blend fruits until smooth. Use immediately, or refrigerate up to 3 days, but warm to room temp ~ 70° F before use.
9. Combine sugar, baking powder, salt, cinnamon, cloves, baking soda, nutmeg, eggs, and vanilla a large bowl.
10. Using a handheld electric mixer set at low speed, to moisten dry ingredients.
11. Then, increase speed to medium and whip until thick and fluffy, about 5 minutes.
12. Add melted butter in a slow, steady stream.

13. Then, reduce speed to low and add the flour – continue to beat until the mixture is smooth.
14. Place cast-iron skillet in the preheated oven to warm it.
15. Add the fruit purée and mix only until well-combined.
16. Fold in the toasted pecans with a rubber spatula, scraping the bowl along the bottom and sides to ensure it is well-blended.
17. Remove cast-iron skillet from oven and spray with PAM.
18. Pour batter evenly into the skillet.
19. Bake in preheated oven for about 45 minutes or until the cake is well-risen and golden brown. A toothpick inserted into the center will have a few crumbs still attached when removed, and your fingertip will leave a slight indentation in the puffy crust.
20. Set on a wire rack until completely cool – at least 90 minutes.
21. Frost the cake with your favorite cream cheese or buttercream frosting (Should take about 2 cups.)
22. Sprinkle toasted pecans across the top.
23. Serve immediately, or leave at room temperature until ready to serve, up to 24 hours at cool room temperature.
24. After cutting, wrap leftover slices individually and store at cool room temperature for up to 2 days.

RECIPE NOTES

- Hummingbird Cake is almost always made as a layer cake; but, a cast-iron skillet dresses it down to more casual. It is also easier to transport and perfect for potlucks and picnics.
- Puréeing the fruit maximizes its flavor more than simply chopping or mashing.
- A pinch of cloves intensifies the banana flavor.
- A 10-inch cast-iron skillet is a perfect size for a casual cake to feed a crowd.

Libby's® Pumpkin Pie

8 Servings – 335 Calories per serving

I have tried many pumpkin pie recipes, and this is by far the easiest and the best pumpkin pie of all – so, "Why mess with success?"

INGREDIENTS

- ¾ cup granulated sugar
- 1 teaspoon ground cinnamon
- ½ teaspoon salt
- ½ teaspoon ground ginger
- ¼ teaspoon ground cloves
- 2 large cage-free eggs
- 1 can (15 oz.) LIBBY'S® 100% Pure Pumpkin
- 1 can (12 oz.) evaporated milk
- 1 unbaked 9-inch Pillsbury™ Refrigerated Pie Crust (or make your own from scratch)
- Freshly whipped cream – lightly sweetened

DIRECTIONS

1. Preheat the oven to 425° F.
2. Follow the directions on the Pillsbury™ Refrigerated Pie Crust to prepare one 9-inch pie crust.
3. Crimp the edges of the crust and set aside.
4. In a small bowl, mix the sugar, cinnamon, salt, ginger, and cloves using a wire whisk to stir.
5. Place the eggs in a large bowl and beat until fluffy.
6. Stir in pumpkin and sugar-spice mixture.
7. Mix all the ingredients until well-blended.
8. Gradually stir in evaporated milk – continue stirring until the mixture is smooth and creamy.
9. Pour into prepared pie shell.
10. Place a pie-crust protector on the pie.
11. Bake in preheated 425° F oven for 15 minutes.
12. Reduce heat to 350° F and continue baking for 40 to 50 minutes or until a knife inserted near the center of the pie comes out clean.
13. Cool on a wire rack for at least 2 hours.
14. Serve immediately or refrigerate.
15. Top each piece with a generous serving of freshly whipped cream before serving.

Sea Salt Caramel Chip Chocolate Brownies

24 Servings – 230 Calories per serving (without caramel drizzle)

Brownies were a common dessert when I was growing up and one of the first desserts I learned to bake. This out-of-the-ordinary version is made with caramel chips, which add a surprising extra flavor burst to this traditional sweet treat.

INGREDIENTS

- 2 cups flour
- ½ cup unsweetened cocoa powder
- 2 cups granulated sugar
- 1 cup butter melted
- 4 large cage-free eggs, room temperature
- 2 teaspoons vanilla extract
- ½ teaspoon cinnamon
- 1 bag (10 ounces) Hershey's Sea Salt Caramel baking chips.
- ¼ cup caramel sundae sauce for drizzling (optional)

DIRECTIONS

1. Preheat oven to 350° F.
2. Generously butter a 9 x 13-inch pan or line with foil or parchment paper, and spray with non-stick cooking spray.
3. Place the flour, cocoa powder, and sugar in a large bowl and whisk until well combined.
4. Add the melted butter, eggs, vanilla extract, and cinnamon.
5. Mix the ingredients using an electric hand-held mixer on medium/low speed for 2-3 minutes – mix only until combined, <u>DO NOT Overmix.</u>

6. Gently fold in the caramel chips with a large wooden spoon.

7. Spread brownie batter into prepared pan.

8. Bake for 25-30 minutes, until a toothpick inserted in the center of the brownies comes out clean.

9. Place on a wire rack to cool for 15 minutes before drizzling with caramel.

World's Best Cheesecake

8 Servings - 368 Calories per serving

This one of my family's favorite desserts - always part of holiday meals and most birthdays. It is also extremely easy to make. It is wonderful served plain. You can also serve with little fruit garnish on top; with crushed, lightly sweetened strawberries; or drizzle with chocolate. Be creative!

INGREDIENTS

For the Crust

- 18 graham crackers, crushed.
- 6 tablespoons butter (no substitutes)
- ¼ cup sugar

Cream Cheese Filling

- 4 three-ounce packages cream cheese, room temperature
- ½ cup sugar
- 2 large eggs
- ½ lemon (juice only) – freshly squeezed

Sour Cream Topping

- ½ pint cup sour cream (1 cup)
- 1 tablespoon sugar
- ½ teaspoon vanilla extract

DIRECTIONS

Make the Crust

1. Preheat the oven to 350° F.
2. Melt butter in the microwave; set aside.
3. Place crackers in a heavy plastic bag and roll with a rolling pin until finely crushed. *(This should be done in small batches)*.
4. Place 1½ cups of the graham crackers crumbs in a medium-sized bowl.
5. Add sugar and mix thoroughly.
6. Stir in the melted butter and mix until well-blended.
7. Press the mixture into a 9" pin plate.
8. Bake for 8 to 10 minutes – let cool while mixing the filling.

Alternate Crust

- Use a packaged prepared graham cracker crust and bake in a hot oven (400° F.) for 5 minutes – set aside to cool.
- This crust works; but. it is not as tasty as the homemade version above.

Make the Cream Cheese Filling

1. With a hand electric mixer, blend the following: cream cheese, sugar, eggs, lemon juice. Mix until smooth.
2. Pour into graham cracker crust.
3. Bake at 350° F. for 25 - 30 minutes – the center should be a little soft (DO NOT OVERCOOK).
4. Cool at least 15 minutes on a wire rack before adding the sour cream topping.

Make the Sour Cream Topping

1. Increase the oven temperature to 400° F.
2. Add 1 tablespoon sugar and ½ teaspoon vanilla to the sour cream and mix well.
3. Spread the topping carefully cover the cream cheese pie. Be sure the topping touches the edges of the crust.
4. Bake 5 to 7 minutes (do not overcook).
5. Cool on wire rack.
6. Cover with Saran Wrap and refrigerate overnight before serving.

CANDY

This group of recipes has a special place in my heart. Not only because I love candy, but because making candy was where my love affair with cooking began.

There was no TV when I was growing up, so on cold, rainy evenings, we often made candy. Also, when I was in high school, it was a fun activity when my girlfriends and I were having sleepovers. *(We called them Slumber Parties.)*

Finally, as a young mother, I enjoyed teaching my girls how to make candy – a family tradition.

Some of the recipes included are from those long-ago times. Classic Divinity and Creamy Chocolate Nut Fudge *(which is a variation on the much more difficult recipe we used)* are at the top of the list, plus many others collected through the years that I think you will enjoy.

252

Creamy Chocolate Nut Fudge

36 Pieces – 146 Calories per piece

This creamy, nutty chocolate fudge can be made in less than 10 minutes. Your family and friends will think you are an amazing cook.

INGREDIENTS

- 2 cups dark chocolate chips (12 oz bag)
- 1 can (14 ounces) sweetened condensed milk
- ¼ cup butter
- 1 teaspoon vanilla extract
- 1 cup chopped pecans plus about 2 tablespoons for topping

DIRECTIONS

1. Butter the bottom of a square baking pan or line it with parchment paper.
2. In a medium-sized glass mixing bowl, mix the chocolate chips, condensed milk, and butter.
3. Heat in the microwave for 90 seconds.
4. Stir the mixture to blend and heat another 25 seconds if chips are not all melted.
5. Add the vanilla extract and stir until smooth; add the chopped pecans.
6. Scoop the chocolate mixture into the prepared pan and spread evenly with a rubber spatula.
7. Top with remaining 2 tablespoons chopped pecans (optional).
8. Let the fudge harden – you may need to place in the fridge for 30 minutes or longer.

9. Cut into 1-inch squares and store in an airtight container in the fridge for a week.

10. Enjoy this delicious treat with friends and family!

RECIPE NOTES

- Nuts are optional. Many people prefer their fudge plain.
- If you prefer, instead of using the microwave you can melt the chocolate, milk, and butter in a double boiler on the top of the stove.

Chocolate Peanut Butter Fudge

30 Pieces – 225 Calories per piece

Chocolate and peanut butter – is there any combination better than that? This recipe creates two melt-in-your-mouth layers of deliciousness - chocolate fudge layered on top of peanut butter fudge. Made in the microwave – so quick and easy, you will be blown away. Because it is irresistibly yummy, it may disappear before it has time to chill completely!

INGREDIENTS

- 1 cup Laura Scudders© Natural SMOOTH Peanut Butter (brand makes a difference)
- 1 cup butter
- 2 teaspoons vanilla divided
- 3½ cups powdered sugar (measure carefully)
- Dash of salt
- 1 small can (7 oz) sweetened condensed milk
- 1½ cups semisweet chocolate chips (12 oz bag is TWO cups)
- 2 tablespoons butter

255

DIRECTIONS

Make the Peanut Butter Fudge

1. Place the peanut butter and butter in a large microwave-safe bowl.
2. Microwave for 1 minute and 30 seconds.
3. Stir well and return to the microwave for another one minute and 30 seconds.
4. When the mixture is blended, add salt and one teaspoon of vanilla.
5. Add the powdered sugar one cup at a time, mixing well after each addition. *(Mixture will be very thick.)*
6. Spread into a buttered 9 X 13-inch baking dish – if you like thicker pieces, use a square baking dish instead.
7. Cover with plastic wrap, and chill in the refrigerator for at least 30 minutes.

After Chilling . . . Make the Chocolate Fudge

8. Place the sweetened condensed milk, chocolate chips, and butter in a microwave-safe bowl,
9. Microwave for one minute – remove from microwave and stir to blend the ingredients.
10. Continue microwaving and stirring in 30-second bursts until the mixture is completely melted and smooth.
11. Stir in the remaining one teaspoon vanilla.
12. Add ½ cup of nuts (optional).
13. Spread the chocolate fudge over the peanut butter fudge.
14. Return to the refrigerator for at least 2 hours – or until set.
15. Cut into 30 pieces.

Classic Divinity

48 Pieces – 31 Calories per piece

The root of the word divinity is divine . . . and that it is! You must try this light, super-sweet, airy candy confection that tastes like Heaven. Divinity is one of the two traditional holiday candies - Chocolate Fudge the other. They make great gifts and are must-haves in our home at Christmas; or, any time I can be convinced to make them.

INGREDIENTS

- 2½ cups granulated sugar
- ½ cup light corn syrup
- ½ cup water
- 2 large cage-free egg whites (cold)
- 1 teaspoon vanilla extract
- ¾ cup pecans, finely chopped (optional)

DIRECTIONS

1. Candy thermometer recommended.

2. Stir sugar, corn syrup, and water (use 1 tablespoon less on very humid days) over low heat until sugar is dissolved.

3. Cook, without stirring to 260° F. on a candy thermometer *(or until a small amount of mixture dropped into very cold water forms a hardball).*

4. While the sugar mixture is cooking, beat the egg whites on high speed using an electric handheld mixer until stiff peaks form.

5. Once the sugar mixture reaches 260°, remove from heat and very slowly pour it in a thin, steady stream over the egg whites while mixing on high speed. It should take about 2 minutes to pour the hot liquid over the egg whites, so pour slowly and don't rush this step.

6. Continue to beat on high speed for another 5-8 minutes until the candy loses some of its glossiness and starts to hold its shape.

7. You can stop mixing and test a small amount of candy by dropping a small spoonful of it onto the parchment paper to see if it holds the shape of a nice rounded mound (which is what you want) or if it melts into a puddle.

8. Continue to beat a minute or two longer if the divinity doesn't hold its shape, test again

9. Mix in the chopped pecans and vanilla when the candy stays in a mound instead of melting into itself.

10. Using two spoons sprayed lightly with cooking spray, drop tablespoon-size scoops of divinity onto the prepared baking sheet, using one spoon to scrape the hot candy off the other spoon. You will want to work quickly while the candy is still hot.

11. Let the candy set, then store for up to 5 days in an airtight container.

RECIPE NOTES

- You can pour the candy into a lightly buttered 9 X 9-inch baking dish, spread it evenly in the pan, and let it set up. Then, cut into squares.

Oreo Chocolate Truffles

36 Truffles – 149 Calories each

Oreo Truffles are the perfect treat for any occasion! They only require THREE ingredients, they couldn't be easier to make, and they taste amazing. They're always the first thing to go at parties, I've yet to meet someone who doesn't love them!

INGREDIENTS

- 36 Oreos (Original), crushed, plus 3 extra for topping if desired
- 1 (8 oz) pkg. cream cheese, softened
- 16 oz vanilla or chocolate candy melts, or melted white chocolate, milk chocolate or dark chocolate
- See notes for peppermint variation

DIRECTIONS

1. Line an 18 X 13-inch cookie sheet with wax paper or parchment paper.
2. Place 36 Oreos in a large resealable bag, seal bag and crush with a rolling pin until finely crushed; set aside.
3. Place softened cream cheese in a large mixing bowl and beat with an electric hand-held mixer until light and fluffy.
4. Slowly mix in crushed Oreos until well combined with the cream cheese.
5. Scoop out the mixture one tablespoon at a time and form into 1-inch balls and place on prepared cookie sheet.
6. Place truffles in the freezer for 15 minutes.

While truffles are chilling . . .

7. Crush remaining 3 Oreos.
8. Melt almond bark or chocolate according to directions on the package.
9. Remove truffles from freezer and dip in melted chocolate – use a spoon to pour some chocolate over the top then lift and allow excess chocolate to run off.
10. Place dipped truffles back onto a baking sheet, immediately sprinkle tops with crushed Oreos if desired, then allow chocolate to set.
11. Store in an airtight container in the refrigerator.

RECIPE NOTES

Peppermint Version

1. Mix 1½ teaspoon of peppermint extract into the cream cheese, then add the Oreo crumbs and continue as directed.
2. Dip chocolates: then, immediately sprinkle tops with peppermint bits, crushed candy canes, or crushed starlight mints (instead of more crushed Oreos).

Quick and Easy Peanut Brittle

Approximately 48 pieces – Calories are difficult to compute because piece size will vary, depending on how it breaks.

This incredibly easy candy was one of my family's favorites. It is an easy, never-fail recipe that you and your friends will enjoy. One batch is never enough. It's great for gifting during the holidays! Be careful making it - you must move quickly once you add the peanuts. The hot candy will set up so fast, it will surprise you. Have fun!

INGREDIENTS
- 2 cups granulated sugar
- ½ cup water
- 1 cup light corn syrup
- 1 dash salt
- 2 cups raw peanuts
- 1 tablespoon butter
- 1 teaspoon vanilla extract
- 1 teaspoon baking soda (heaping teaspoon)

DIRECTIONS

1. Candy thermometer recommended.
2. Generously butter two cookie sheets and set aside.
3. In a heavy-duty saucepan, mix the following: 2 cups sugar, ½ cup water, 1 cup corn syrup, and a dash of salt
4. Bring to boil, without stirring and cook to hard ball stage *(296° F – candy thermometer)*. Watch the thermometer closely – it doesn't take long.
5. Remove the thermometer.
6. Add raw peanuts, 1 tablespoon butter, and 1 teaspoon vanilla – continue boiling, stirring constantly until golden brown and smells like peanut brittle *(big bubbles start puffing up)*.
7. Remove from heat and add 1 heaping teaspoon baking soda, stir to foaming *(at least one full stir)*.
8. Pour onto cookie sheets. Be quick, you must pour extremely fast! Do not scrape the pan
9. Let cool and break into pieces - makes ~48 pieces

CHRISTMAS COOKIES

You have probably helped your mom, your grandmothers, or some other family member or friend to make Christmas Cookies. If you haven't, now is your chance to enjoy the adventure.

The best part is that none of them are difficult to make. All you need are good recipes *(which you now have),* the right ingredients, and the happy holiday spirit.

Invite friends over to enjoy the holidays by making Christmas classics like, Shortbread Cookies that you can decorate with festive-colored frosting and sprinkles. And, be sure to make Gingerbread Cookies, for the children you love.

I think it is more fun when friends join you; but I love making cookies so much that I never let being alone stop me from embracing this holiday tradition. The Peanut Butter Blossoms are my favorite, and sooooo easy!

Classic Shortbread Cookies

36 Cookies – 228 Calories each cookie

Classic Shortbread Cookies are made with only three ingredients.
They are mouthwatering, buttery, and melt-in-your-mouth delicious.
This is a classic holiday cookie, made two ways!

INGREDIENTS
- 1½ cups (3 sticks) salted butter, softened to room temperature
- 1 cup powdered (confectioner's) sugar
- 3 cups all-purpose flour

DIRECTIONS
1. Preheat oven to 325° F.
2. Line an ungreased cookie sheet with parchment paper.
3. Allow some parchment paper to hang off the sides of the pan for easy lifting once the cookies are baked.
4. Using a hand-held electric mixer on medium speed, whip the butter in a large bowl until fluffy *(about 30 seconds)*.
5. Add the powdered sugar and continue mixing until well blended.
6. Scrape down the sides of the bowl and mix-in completely.
7. Add flour and mix at low speed until well blended. *(The mixture will be crumbled and soft.)*
8. Pat dough into an ungreased cookie sheet, lined with parchment paper.

   As an alternative:
   - Roll out the dough to ¼-inch thickness.
   - Knead just enough for the dough to hold together, but don't overwork it.
   - Then cut into your desired shape.

9. Bake for 12 to 15 minutes, or until just done *(slightly golden)*. Do not let them get brown.
10. Remove from the oven.
11. If using a cookie sheet, lift out the cookies from the sheet using the parchment paper and cut into desired shapes.
12. Finish cooling the cookies on a rack.

RECIPE NOTES

- If you use butter as listed, salt is not required unless you use unsalted butter. Then, add ¼ teaspoon salt to the recipe.
- Choose your style: divide the dough in half.
    - Bake half in an 8 X 8-inch baking pan lined with parchment paper.
    - Roll out the other half and cut with a cookie cutter.
    - Then, you can see which style you prefer.
- Cookies can be frozen in an airtight container for up to three months, which makes them easy to bake ahead for the holidays. Just thaw and serve as is, or frost to make them more festive.

Easy Sprinkle Cookies

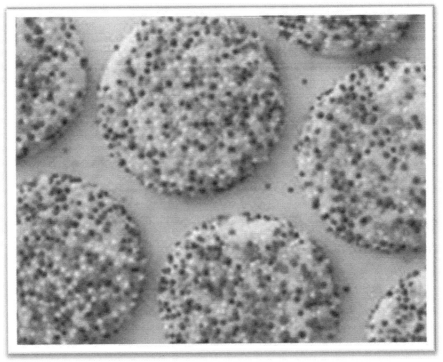

36 Cookies – 92 Calories per cookie

The child in all of us loves sprinkles – especially when they are sprinkled on soft, sweet sugar cookies. This recipe is so easy to make that you will want to use it during the holidays for every child you know and love (including yourself). You can change the sprinkle colors to match every holiday or just for fun.

INGREDIENTS

- 2½ cups flour
- 1 teaspoon baking powder
- ¼ teaspoon baking soda
- ½ teaspoon salt
- 1 cup unsalted butter, softened (not melted)
- 1¼ cups sugar

- 2 oz cream cheese, softened
- 1 large egg
- 1 teaspoon vanilla
- ½ teaspoon almond extract
- ¾ - 1 cup sprinkles (nonpareils, jimmies or colored sugar sprinkles)

DIRECTIONS

1. Preheat oven to 350° F.
2. Line baking sheets with parchment paper.
3. Place sprinkles in a small mixing bowl; set aside.
4. Whisk the flour, baking powder, baking soda, and salt until well mixed; set aside.
5. Using a hand-held electric mixer – blend the butter, sugar, and cream cheese.
6. Mix in egg, vanilla, and almond extracts.
7. Stir in the flour mixture and continue to stir until well combined. *(If you live in a very humid climate, you may need to chill dough for at least 30 minutes or it may be too sticky to create the cookie balls.)*
8. Scoop dough out 1½ tablespoons at a time – a cookie scoop works well for this.
9. Shape the dough into balls and roll in the sprinkles.
10. Place on a prepared baking sheet about 2-inches apart.
11. With the bottom of a cup or glass, flatten cookies about halfway.
12. Bake one sheet at a time in the preheated oven, about 9 minutes *(cookies should appear slightly under-baked)*.
13. Cool slightly on the baking sheet and transfer to a wire rack to cool completely.
14. Store cookies in an airtight container.

Gingerbread Cookies

24 cookies – 229 calories each

This Gingerbread Cookie recipe makes perfectly soft and chewy cookies and with just the right amount of spices and rich molasses flavor. The dough is easy to work with and they are fun to decorate. These will quickly become a new favorite holiday cookie!

INGREDIENTS

Cookies

- 3 cups flour
- 1 tablespoon ground ginger
- 2 teaspoons ground cinnamon
- ¼ teaspoon ground cloves
- ¼ teaspoon ground nutmeg
- ¾ teaspoon baking powder
- ½ teaspoon baking soda
- ½ teaspoon salt

271

- ¾ cup packed dark brown sugar
- 10 tablespoons unsalted butter, softened
- 1 egg yolk (large)
- 1½ teaspoons vanilla extract
- ½ cup molasses (not blackstrap)
- 1 - 2 tablespoons milk

Royal Icing for Decorating
- 3 cups powdered sugar
- 1½ tablespoons meringue powder
- 4 - 6 tablespoons water
- ¼ teaspoon vanilla extract

DIRECTIONS
1. Preheat oven to 350° F.

Make the Cookies
2. In a mixing bowl whisk the flour, ginger, cinnamon, cloves, nutmeg, baking powder, baking soda, and salt; set aside.
3. Using a hand-held electric mixer, cream sugar and butter until well combined. Be sure to scrape down the sides of the bowl several times as you mix.
4. Add the egg yolk and vanilla.
5. Mix in molasses and 1 tablespoon milk.
6. With the mixer on low speed, slowly add dry ingredients and mix until combined. Add just enough additional milk as needed to hold the dough together.
7. Divide dough into two equal portions.
8. Place dough between two sheets of parchment paper and roll out each portion evenly to ¼-inch thickness (preferably into an oblong or rectangular shape so it will fit on a cookie sheet).

272

9. Place the cookie sheet in the freezer 10 - 20 minutes to chill.

10. When the dough is firm, cut into shapes with cookie cutters.

11. Remove each cookie from paper using a thin metal spatula or pastry scraper, if needed.

12. Transfer to parchment paper-lined cookie sheet, spacing cookies about 1-inch apart.

13. Bake in preheated oven for ~8 minutes or until slightly set.

14. Remove from oven and cool on baking sheet ~2 minutes; then, transfer to a wire rack to cool completely.

15. Repeat process with remaining dough.

Make the Royal Icing

16. Place powdered sugar and meringue powder in a medium mixing bowl.

17. Using a hand-held electric mixer on low speed, add 4 tablespoons water and the vanilla until well-combined.

18. Add more water to thin as needed and increase speed; whip the mixture until it is glossy and thick.

19. Separate into bowls and tint with food coloring, if desired.

20. Transfer to piping bags fitted with tiny round tips or into Ziploc sandwich bags with a corner cut off.

21. Decorate cookies with icing and add sprinkles if desired.

22. Let icing set at room temperature until set and store in an airtight container.

RECIPE NOTES

- Be sure to use the *Royal Icing* Recipe that is included. If you use regular buttercream frosting, your results will not be what you want them to be.

- Softened butter should be soft but still holds its shape well. The cool butter will make the dough easier to work with and the cookies will not spread so much.
- When you **test the cookies for doneness**, there should be a slight indentation when touched. For soft cookies, be careful not to over-bake. If you prefer crisp cookies, bake them a little longer.
- Cookies are softer the second day, which I think makes them better.

Peanut Butter Blossoms

30 Cookies – 143 Calories each cookie

Soft peanut butter cookies with a chocolate kiss in the center. Everyone LOVES these peanut butter cookies! They are easy-peasy to make and will disappear quickly.

INGREDIENTS

- 1¾ cups all-purpose flour
- 1 teaspoon baking soda
- ½ teaspoon salt
- ½ cup unsalted butter, at room temperature

- ½ cup creamy peanut butter
- 1 cup granulated sugar divided
- ½ cup packed light brown sugar
- 1 large egg
- 1 tablespoon milk
- 1 teaspoon pure vanilla extract
- 30 Hershey's Chocolate Kisses, unwrapped and frozen

DIRECTIONS

1. In a medium bowl, whisk the flour, baking soda, and salt; set aside.
2. Using a stand mixer or hand mixer, cream the butter, peanut butter, ½ cup granulated sugar, and brown sugar until smooth, scraping down the side of the bowl if necessary.
3. Add the egg, milk, and vanilla extract. Beat until combined.
4. Add the flour mixture and mix on low until just combined. Don't over mix.
5. Wrap the dough in plastic wrap and chill in the refrigerator for at least 30 minutes. It can be chilled for up to 72 hours.
6. Place the Hershey's Kisses in the freezer so they are frozen when you put them on the cookies. This will help the kisses to keep their shape and not melt.
7. When ready to bake, preheat oven to 350° F.
8. Line a large baking sheet with a Silpat baking mat or parchment paper.
9. Roll the peanut butter cookie dough into balls, about 1 tablespoon of dough per cookie.
10. Place the remaining ½ cup sugar in a small bowl.
11. Roll the cookie dough balls in the sugar until they are generously coated.

12. Place the cookie dough balls onto the prepare baking sheet, about 2 inches apart.
13. Bake the cookies until they start to crack on the edges, about 8 or 9 minutes.
14. Remove the baking sheet from the oven and lightly press a frozen chocolate kiss into the center of each cookie, allowing it to crack slightly.
15. Return to oven and bake for an additional 2 minutes.
16. Remove from the oven and let the cookies cool on the baking sheet for 2 to 3 minutes.
17. Transfer to a cooling rack and cool until the kisses harden.
18. If you want to speed up the process, you can put the cookies in the freezer so the kisses will harden faster.
19. Cookies can be stored in an airtight container for up to four days *(if they last that long).*

Raspberry Almond Shortbread Thumbprint Cookies

36 cookies – 117 calories each

These Raspberry Almond Shortbread Thumbprint Cookies are simply delicious and should have a place of honor on your holiday cookie tray!

INGREDIENTS

- 2 cups + 2 tablespoons flour*
- ¼ teaspoon salt
- 1 cup unsalted butter, cold and diced into pieces
- 2/3 cup granulated sugar
- ½ teaspoon almond extract
- ½ cup seedless raspberry jam

DIRECTIONS

Make the Cookies

1. Preheat oven to 350° F.
2. In a mixing bowl whisk the flour and salt until thoroughly mixed – set aside.
3. Using an electric hand-held mixer, whip the butter and sugar until combined *(it will take a minute or two since the butter is cold).*
4. Stir in almond extract.
5. Add dry ingredients and blend until the mixture comes together *(the mixture will be dry and crumbly at first, continue to mix until blended).*
6. Make 1-inch balls from the dough *(~1 tablespoon each),* and place 2-inches apart on ungreased baking sheets.
7. Make a small indentation with thumb or forefinger in each cookie *(just large enough for ¼ to ½ teaspoon of jam).*
8. Fill each indentation with jam.
9. Chill prepared cookies in the refrigerator for 20 minutes *(or freezer for 10 minutes).*
10. Bake in preheated oven 14 - 18 minutes.
11. Cool several minutes on the baking sheet then, transfer to a wire rack to cool.
12. Store cookies in an airtight container until ready to serve.

RECIPE NOTES

- Scoop flour with a measuring cup and cut and then, level with a table knife.
- Do not whisk or sift first and don't spoon flour into the measuring cup.

About the Author

Nancy N. Wilson is a writer, blogger, and bestselling author of more than 30 books – over half are cookbooks.

She was born and reared in a small farming community in Southern Arizona. She earned a B.S. Degree in Education and Psychology at Utah State University and an MBA at Thunderbird School of Global Management.

Her one constant lifetime companion has been cooking, which began as a young child when her mother gave her free rein in the kitchen to create masterpieces of flour, sugar, spices, and anything else she could find in the cupboards.

When she finally learned to follow a recipe, Mexican food and a wide variety of desserts (including cookies) were her two favorite types of foods to prepare.

Growing up in a small town in the 50s and 60s gave her many free hours to experiment and master the craft. She especially enjoyed cooking for her friends.

Even with college, marriage, and all the adventures of life, her love of cooking never faltered. She was always looking for new recipes and new creative touches for traditional dishes. She cooked her way through years of marriage, a divorce, and a multi-faceted career,

She has lived and worked on both the East Coast and West Coast of the United States, consulted with major corporations in Europe and Japan, and traveled extensively throughout Central and South America.

In 2007, she returned to Arizona to live near her two sons and to do what she has always wanted to do – WRITE.

She now spends her time contributing to her "Healthy Living Blog, (https://Mamaslegacycookbooks.com), testing new recipes, and writing and publishing non-fiction books – half of which are cookbooks.

She finds great satisfaction and joy in sharing all she has learned with you, her readers, and hopes that you will benefit and develop a passion for cooking as great or greater than hers.

Other Books by This Author

Mama's Legacy Series
Seven Volumes Available

Dinner – 55 Easy Recipes (Volume I)

Breakfast and Brunch – 60 Delicious Recipes (Volume II)

Dessert – 50 Scrumptious Recipes (Volume III)

Chicken – 25 Classic Dinners (Volume IV)

Mexican Favorites – 21 Traditional Recipes (Volume V)

Side Dishes – 60 Great Recipes (Volume VI)

Sauce Recipes – 50 Tasty Choices (Volume VII)

Other Cookbooks

Candy Making Made Easy - Instructions and 17 Starter Recipes

Cake Making Made Easy - Instructions and 60 Cakes

Cook Ahead – Freezer to Table

Garden Fresh Soups and Stews

Juicing for Life – The Secret to Vibrant Health

SPECIAL DIETS Fresh and Easy Cookbook

Sweet Treats – Candy, Cookies, Cake, Ice Cream, Pudding, and Pie

Tweens and Teens – A Cookbook to Get You Started

COOKIES! The Best Collection of Cookie Recipes EVER! Just for YOU!

Health and Fitness/Gardening

DETOX – The Master Cleanse Diet

Growing Tomatoes – Everything You Need to Know, and More

Growing Roses – The Beginner's Handbook

Stop Eating Yourself into an Early Grave

WOW! You Look Fantastic!

Business

Books Written under Pseudonyms

Made in the USA
Middletown, DE
09 December 2021

54864631R10166